HOW TO WRITE YOUR WAY TO SUCCESS IN BUSINESS

Dianna Booher

BARNES & NOBLE BOOKS

A DIVISION OF HARPER & ROW, PUBLISHERS

New York, Cambridge, Philadelphia
San Francisco, London, Mexico City
São Paulo, Singapore, Sydney

HOW TO WRITE YOUR WAY TO SUCCESS IN BUSINESS. Copyright © 1983 by Dianna Booher. All rights reserved. Printed in the United States of America. No part of this book may be used or reproduced in any manner whatsoever without written permission except in the case of brief quotations embodied in critical articles and reviews. For information address Facts on File Publications, 460 Park Avenue South, New York, NY 10016. Published simultaneously in Canada by Fitzhenry & Whiteside Limited, Toronto.

First BARNES & NOBLE BOOKS edition published 1984.

Library of Congress Cataloging in Publication Data

Booher, Dianna Daniels.
  How to write your way to success in business.

  (Everyday handbook; EH/597)
  Reprint. Originally published: Would you put that in writing? New York, N.Y.: Facts on File, c1983.
  Bibliography: p.
  1. English language—Rhetoric.   2. English language—Business English.
I. Title.
PE1479.B87B66 1984   808'.066651   84-47557
ISBN 0-06-463597-X (pbk.)

84 85 86 87 88 10 9 8 7 6 5 4 3 2 1

A Note to the Reader

Assuming that one sample is worth a thousand words, I have written this book as a business report. The beginning section contains the summary, conclusions, and recommendations. (You may stop reading after that section and have a "photo" of the entire book's contents—but please don't.) The middle section discusses these conclusions and recommendations in detail. The appendixes contain examples and quizzes to supplement the main body of information.

One difference in this book and an actual business report, however, is the tone. Because my subject is complex and because you are not a captive reader, I've tried to keep the tone light and informal.

DIANNA BOOHER

CONTENTS

APPENDIXES

FIGURES

SUMMARY, CONCLUSIONS, AND RECOMMENDATIONS

Effective business writing requires training; success comes by method, not chance. Because communication involves more than one person, readers, writers and typists have legitimate complaints about the reports, letters, and memos that cross their desks. Here's how participants from my writing workshops have voiced their frustrations:

Writers' Complaints

- I never know exactly what approach my supervisor wants.
- My boss doesn't tell me why a report or letter was rejected. And when he asks me to revise, he doesn't give specific suggestions.
- I can't find good writing samples to follow, and setting up new formats takes time.
- I'm fuzzy on grammatical points.
- I don't like to write, so it's difficult for me.
- My supervisor is on an ego trip when he edits my work; everything has to be said his way.
- I spend too much time trying to decide how to start.
- I never know how detailed to get and what I can assume my reader knows.

Readers' Complaints

- The writer doesn't get to the point soon enough.
- Organization is muddled; I have to dig out the main ideas.

1

- What the writer assumes is obvious, is not.
- I can't tell exactly what the writer wants me to do.
- There's too much hedging and avoiding the issue.
- The writer keeps repeating himself.
- I have to get out the thesaurus to read some writers.
- The writing is too formal and sounds silly.
- The tone causes an adverse gut reaction.

Typists' Complaints

- My supervisor waits until the very last minute to give me the work for typing; I'm too rushed to check punctuation or spelling.
- I can't read my supervisor's handwriting.
- I type for several people and they're all inconsistent with their editorial marks.
- I'm never sure what changes I'm expected to make.
- Sometimes I see errors, but my supervisor doesn't think I know what I'm talking about. It's hard to keep quiet when you know things are unclear or grammatically incorrect. Pointing out errors is sometimes threatening to the writer.

The burden for untangling these communication wires falls on you, the writer. Educators know that if the student has not learned, the teacher has not taught. The same is true in the communication process. If the reader has not understood your message, you have not written well.

OBJECTIVES IN BUSINESS WRITING

The business writer has one major concern and that is to be effective, to accomplish a purpose. That purpose may be to get action, to inform, or merely to create goodwill. Clarity, conciseness, and favorable image promote that end result. And achieving these objectives—clarity, conciseness, and favorable image— necessarily accomplishes the fourth objective, cost-efficiency.

CLARITY

Misunderstandings anger people, cost money, and even endanger lives. A supervisor writes, "Anyone wishing to file for these benefits should report to Room 222 at three o'clock." He then reprimands an ineligible employee who shows up at the meeting. If the supervisor didn't make clear *which* employees were entitled to the benefits, his reprimand embarrasses and angers the employee who has misunderstood.

A similar misunderstanding with a client can lose an account. "Delivery of an additional vacuum pump and porta-power will be required for the project, which has been postponed pending SOC approval." What has been postponed? The delivery? Or the project?

When someone needs "twelve-foot long pipes" and instead orders "twelve foot-long pipes," he too has unnecessarily decreased company profits on the construction job. Even if the incorrect shipment can be returned, consider the shipping costs and lost time involved in the mix-up.

Similarly, instructions like the following from a safety manual may be the basis for a lawsuit by an injured employee:

> When motors or controllers operating at more than 150 volts to ground are guarded against accidental contact only by location, and where adjustment or other attendance may be necessary during operations, suitable insulating mats or platforms shall be provided. All belts, pulleys, chains, flywheels, shafting and shaft projections, or other rotating or reciprocating parts within seven feet of the floor or working platform shall be effectively guarded.

Can you dig out the two safety precautions to be taken? What specifically is "effectively guarded"? Is using the mats a choice or a company regulation? And if using the mats is a company regulation, who is responsible to see that such regulations are followed? The operator himself? The project supervisor? A lawsuit may be necessary to find out.

The stakes in unclear writing can be high.

CONCISENESS

A concise memo, letter, or report saves reading time, writing time, and secretarial time—not to mention paper. Says one field supervisor, "When I glance down and see the signature, I want to throw the memo back in my 'in' basket until I have a full day to devote to it. No matter what the subject, he rambles on and on and on. I just don't have the time."

Top-management readers agree. The most frequent complaint I hear from these readers is that their staffs do not know how to get to the main points quickly; these managers continually struggle to keep on top of the reading piled on their desks for review and/or approval.

In addition to savings in time and money, conciseness enhances clarity; main points stand out rather than fade into a collage of details.

PERSONAL AND COMPANY IMAGE

Clients often evaluate a company's capability and dependability from its written communications. A technical editor in a natural-gas company reported that his company's bid for a multibillion-dollar job was accepted over other bids for one reason: The client, who had learned English as a second language, was impressed that this company's proposal was the only one without grammatical error. Unfortunately, that client's comment and bid acceptance did not get the technical editor a raise. Management chalked up the incident to a quirk in a picayune buyer.

My research, however, into this area of company image suggests that such decisions are more frequent than poor writers would like to believe. When a report or letter writer is careless in his writing, how can a client know for sure that he's more careful with data or money?

Clients notice errors. They either smile and overlook them, become vexed at what seems like little concern for their business, or get downright angry if either tone or clarity is the problem.

Poor writing not only affects company image but also limits personal promotions within the company. A manager of industrial relations at Dresser Industries comments: "Many talented men in our organization who know the business well are overlooked for promotions simply because they cannot communicate well and influence effectively. To manage well, they *must* communicate well. It's a real problem."

Like it or not, writing characterizes.

WRITING CHARACTERIZES

COST-EFFICIENCY

If you've never figured the cost of poor writing as well as the savings in good writing, use the following guidelines to personalize time or cost for your company:

READING COSTS

200 words/minute	average reading time for business materials
10-page report	5,000 words or 25 minutes
salary of reader	$40,000/year or $20/hour
reading 10-page report	$8.33
reading cost/year (two reports/day)	$4,165 per reading executive

If this "reading" executive asks for revisions in half the reports submitted to him, he increases his reading cost to $6,248 per year. Multiply this cost by the number of report-reading executives in your company to get an idea of the total reading cost.

And notice that this cost is figured on the assumption that a ten-page report is necessary. If a ten-page report could be more concisely written in five pages, the savings would be even more substantial:

WRITING COSTS

salary of writer	$30,000/year or $15/hour
40 hours/10-page report	$600/10-page report
or:	
spends 35% of time writing	$10,500 writing costs/year/writer

To adapt these figures to your company, survey the various departments—engineering, sales, personnel, accounting, and research and development—for estimates of how much time employees spend writing.

When writers habitually use the principles of good writing, they can cut writing time for most reports or letters by 25 to 50 percent. For instance, if the above $30,000-per-year writer could get his report in final form in half the time he now spends, he could save his company $5,250 per year.

REPRODUCTION COSTS

Per-page cost for reproduction varies from company to company depending on the existence of an editorial staff, average number of copies made, salary of reproduction clerks, and equipment used. One manager of a large engineering firm *without* an editorial department figures per-page reproduction cost for the average report at $14. Thus, the following figures:

$14/page (based on 30 copies) $\times$ 10 $-$ page report $=$ $1.40

If this "average" report is revised, it must then be reproduced the second time—wasting $140. Multiply this wasted $140 by the number of revised reports per year in your company for an estimate of reproduction loss due to poor writing. And, of course, if a writer cuts report length, he or she has further cut reproduction costs.

Simply put, poor writing costs money; good writing represents a substantial savings.

OBSTACLES TO REACHING THE OBJECTIVES

To be a good communicator, a business writer often must shed old myths and ineffective advice to form new habits.

LAZY THINKING

Many reports, letters, or memos are poorly written because the author does his thinking on paper. He has not considered the total project, interpreted it, and tailored it to his reader's purpose. Often the first few paragraphs or first few pages constitute a warm-up drill. The writer pours out everything on the paper and then comes to a conclusion as he writes through the details. Or worse still, he never comes to a conclusion but rather leaves the conclusion and interpretations for his reader.

POOR MODELS

Poor writing abounds everywhere—in books, magazines, technical journals, newspapers. Company libraries bulge with ineffectively written reports. Too often business writers use ungrammatical constructions, inappropriate words, and a stilted style in their work on the assumption that if a certain usage appeared in print somewhere, it must be acceptable. Not so.

Never assume that because you've seen a certain word used in an unusual way, such usage is an acceptable new trend.

POOR ACADEMIC TRAINING

Yes, even training from English teachers can be at fault. Many English teachers specialize in literature, to the exclusion of writing. Simply because college English majors were required to write *more* compositions than math majors doesn't mean they wrote well or received critique on writing skills. These majors who turn into high-school English teachers may simply be passing on bad advice or perpetuating their own weaknesses in their students' work.

Second, some teachers lack the knowledge or fail to see the necessity of helping students bridge the gap from "academic" writing to business writing. For example, most "academic" reports begin with an introduction and lead to a conclusion. Additionally, academic writing is meant to impress either a teacher or a peer. But in business writing, reports begin with conclusions and seldom need introductions, and business writers' chief purpose is to express rather than impress.

Finally, some teachers may inadvertently encourage poor writing when the purpose of their assignments or advice is unclear. For instance, some advise students to avoid forms of the verb "to be"—is, are, was, were. Generally, that's good advice. "To be" verbs sound weak; stronger verbs add zip. But students sometimes miss the point of this advice about the value of strong verbs. Instead they write awkward sentences to avoid the "to be" construction.

Some teachers also encourage students to build a large vocabulary and often give bonus points for using big words from their weekly vocabulary list. Granted, an extensive vocabulary is to be valued, but a business writer needs to choose words that will be widely understood by all his readers.

Additionally, some teachers encourage student writers to use long sentences. Their motive is admirable—to teach variety in sentence structure: simple, compound, complex, compound-complex. But in a proposal for a joint oil exploration venture, this advice surfaced in the following way:

> Each company agrees that, during each accounting period after the completion date, its Company Throughput which constitutes Initial Facility Throughput, together with such company's Initial Facility Percentage of Initial Facility Throughput during such accounting period which is not Company Throughput, shall be not less than such Company's Initial Facility Percentage of the aggregate of CO_2 which will, at Universal's published tariff rates, which along with other cash resources of the partnership, will be

sufficient to provide, and will actually provide, Universal during such an accounting period with an aggregate amount of cash at least sufficient to avoid a cash deficiency.

An accountant who returned to college after several years in the business world had a professor ask him after the first written assignment, "Would you like me to teach you to write longer sentences?"

"I'd rather not," the accountant answered. "I'd just have to break the habit when I get back on the job." He knows.

The advice to students to build a large vocabulary and vary sentence structure should be tempered with caution about indiscriminate use in the business world. The purpose behind many writing tips has been misunderstood, only to plague the business writer later.

Another academic "contribution" to poor writing is the writer's tendency to assume a captive audience. College professors must read papers to give grades. Often they overlook matters of clarity and gaps in logic because they are familiar with the student's subject and "know what he was trying to say." Clients and colleagues are not so accommodating.

Still another holdover from academic training is equating length with quality. Who hasn't had a teacher who listed expectations for written reports in the form of length rather than content: "I expect a six-to-eight-page critique of your research"? The Declaration of Independence set up a whole new concept of freedom in less than fourteen hundred words. Writers should never confuse quantity with quality.

Writing skills should be taught with careful attention to purpose.

HEDGING AND JARGON

Hedge words and jargon, diseases running rampant in the corporate world, either cover up for a lack of something to say or obscure responsibility when something controversial is said:

> The efficiency with which an operation utilizes its available equipment is an influential factor in productivity. (Efficient use of equipment influences productivity. Is this such a profound idea?)

> It is recognized that there may be no viable alternative to an increased return on total capitalization other than outright purchase. (*Who* recognizes? *May* be no viable alternative?)

Rather than take a stand, these writers attempt to write vaguely and hope no one understands enough to ask questions or to realize that nothing has been said.

INSUFFICIENT TIME FOR EDITING

With poor writers, the first and final drafts are, unfortunately, the same. To most professional writers, real writing is rewriting. Ernest Hemingway is said to have revised *Farewell to Arms* 39 times. Certainly, I'm not advocating such elaborate editing and revising in business memos, letters, or reports, but rarely does a piece of writing of any length require no editing.

Failure to budget time to let your work cool off and then undergo objective editing frequently results in an ill-prepared final copy and time on the phone to interpret, explain, or answer questions about omitted details.

PSEUDO-INTELLECTUALISM

A final reason for poor writing stems from the notion that a heavy style suggests intelligence. Whether a conscious or unconscious phenomenon, writers often slip into an altogether different frame of mind when they pick up the pen. Rather than writing intelligent, clear prose, they turn out what writing analyst Robert Gunning labeled "fog."

When I explain my writing program to a businessman or businesswoman, he or she will comment to a supervisor, "I'd sure like to enroll in this workshop to improve my writing." (12 words) If the supervisor agrees, he usually asks the employee to put the request in writing. The writer then shifts into "writing voice," and the end product is something like the following:

> Because the upgrading of technical expertise in numerous job-related skills is incumbent on each professional in the business world and due to the desirability of a good company and personal

image effected by a writing style which employs clarity, conciseness, and proper tone for enhancement of each written message, it is proposed that my completion of this business writing workshop would be a practical, economical, and efficient method of facilitating these educational and public-relations objectives. (77 words)

"To write simply is as difficult as to be good," said Somerset Maugham. Many writers, however, are afraid no one else knows that. To them, their ability to dazzle with lengthy sentences and big words reveals intelligence.

During a workshop session after I'd quoted Maugham, a vice president of operations asked, "Does everyone know that?"

"Know what?" I asked.

"That if you write in short sentences and use simple words, you're still intelligent."

Here was a writer who, from the expression on his face and the sincerity in his tone, considered writing his vehicle for impressing colleagues and clients with his intelligence. Just the opposite was true. The president of the company had told me earlier in confidence that he had insisted on his vice president's attendance in the workshop: "Mike really knows his field. He generates more business around here than any four men we have on staff. If he could just put his ideas on paper."

Clear writing demands that the writer sort through gobbledygook, elevate the major ideas, subordinate the minor ideas, and eliminate unnecessary details altogether. Intelligence and creativity should be evident in clearly expressed ideas, not in complexly written prose. Translating difficult material into easily understood language requires much skill.

FIVE STEPS FOR EFFECTIVE WRITING

Whatever the reasons for your writing weaknesses, you can become an effective business writer by following the five steps below:

STEP ONE: CONSIDER YOUR AUDIENCE FOR THE PROPER ANGLE

Decide how your reader or readers will use your report, and narrow your message to his or their interests. Choose details to be included on the basis of the audience's experience and knowledge of your subject.

STEP TWO: ANTICIPATE SPECIAL PROBLEMS IN YOUR READER'S REACTION

If you think the reader will be skeptical because of the data you cite or the policies you advocate, or if you foresee a personality or situational problem in the reader's accepting your message, deal with the problem up front. Usually this means refuting alternatives and supporting your conclusions with additional evidence and authority.

STEP THREE: OUTLINE YOUR MESSAGE FUNCTIONALLY

Think before you write. Summarize your entire message in two or three sentences at most. Decide what action your reader needs to take or what action you plan to take. Answer who, when, where, why, how details.

Next, expand this basic outline into some logical format. Begin with a random list of ideas, then shuffle your ideas into a logical order—chronological, geographical, most-to-least significant, categorical, or some other arrangement.

Give your reader the conclusions and recommendations first; follow with a discussion of the hows and the whys of your conclusions and recommendations; last, attach supplementary information in an appendix.

Finally, query your supervisor about your writing plan to see if he agrees with your angle and interpretations. If he doesn't, make the necessary changes in this outline stage.

STEP FOUR: DEVELOP THE FIRST DRAFT

Either compose the report, letter, or memo at the typewriter or dictate it; do not write it in longhand. As you develop this first draft, do not stop to edit and polish grammar but rather concentrate on the logical flow of ideas.

STEP FIVE: EDIT FOR CONTENT, GRAMMAR, CLARITY, CONCISENESS, AND STYLE

Use the following checklists as guides to a polished, well-written final draft:

Content

- Is the angle narrow and consistent?
- Does proportion match emphasis?
- Check accuracy and completeness; add authority.
- Eliminate repetitious details, but retain first-choice words.
- Paragraph by idea and for eye appeal.
- Use informative headings and adequate white space.

Grammar

- Thou shalt not dangle verbals.
- Thou shalt not write fragments for sentences.
- Thou shalt use parallel structure.
- Thou shalt make pronouns agree with their antecedents.
- Thou shalt make verbs agree with their subjects.
- Thou shalt not change tenses and moods unnecessarily.
- Thou shalt punctuate correctly.
- Thou shalt use appropriate words.
- Thou shalt spell correctly.
- Thou shalt not capitalize without a reason.

Clarity

- Measure readability.
- Position to indicate emphasis.
- Link to show proper relationship.
- Use clear transitions.
- Use clear references.
- Place modifiers correctly.
- Prefer concrete words and phrases.
- Use a consistent viewpoint.

Conciseness

- Prefer active voice verbs.
- Dig out buried verbs.
- Avoid adjective and adverb clutter.
- Cut circumlocutions (cliches, redundancies, little-word padding, weak-verb padding).

Style

- Vary sentence structure and length.
- Revise weak verbs.
- Prefer a personal, conversational tone.

DISCUSSION OF THE FIVE STEPS FOR EFFECTIVE WRITING

The most difficult part of writing is getting a handle on the project. Every time I tackle a new book, I feel as if I'm looking at a flopping catfish at the end of my fishing line. The fish just hangs there, flopping back and forth, daring me to catch and unhook him without getting finned. Hovering in exactly the right position, I have to pin the fins firmly to its side before working the hook out of its mouth and feeling it's all mine.

So it is with writing. A well-written letter, memo, or report brings great satisfaction, but the process is usually the pain.

Following this step-by-step plan will help you get a handle on any writing project. Every step has a reason. If you decide to take a shortcut, you'll find the omission will cost you much more time somewhere later in the process.

STEP ONE: CONSIDER YOUR AUDIENCE FOR THE PROPER ANGLE

When writing a report, letter, or memo, always make the reader's interest central. And remember that for the most part, he or she does not care about your trouble, only your results.

WILL THERE BE A SINGLE READER OR MULTIPLE READERS?

Name names. Most all reports and many letters and memos go *through* several persons for approval. And even if the report doesn't need the approval of others, it is often passed on simply to inform them.

When writing to a mixed audience, first rank readers in importance. Then broaden your report or memo to include all levels of readers and their diverse interests in your subject. List names or at least groups of readers your work needs to satisfy: top management; general professional staff, such as engineers, accountants, and geologists; specialists in one particular field such as inspectors, machine operators, auditors, etc.

After you have pinpointed and ranked each reader or group of readers, you should give the most important readers their information first.

When you are writing to only one person, focus solely on *his* likes, dislikes, expectations, or needs.

WHAT ARE THE INTERESTS OF YOUR AUDIENCE?

Management will be interested in answers to the following questions: What is the report's significance? Have we made some major technological advance? What is the profit picture? Are we in compliance with a particular governmental regulation? What about company image? What actions should we take? Who should take these actions?

Note that this kind of information is usually headed "Conclusions and Recommendations."

As the following chart (Figure 1) shows, the majority of managers will read no further into your report or memo.

General professional people will be interested in answers to the following questions: Why was the project undertaken? Why was the policy reevaluated? How did you carry out the research? Under what conditions did you investigate? Are there exceptions to your message? Note that this information is usually given in the "Body" or "Discussion" part of your report or memo.

Specialists will be interested in your detailed evidence—the

HOW MANAGERS READ REPORTS*

Summary	100% of the time
Introduction	65% of the time
Body	22% of the time
Conclusions	55% of the time
Appendix	15% of the time

Study done by Westinghouse Electric Corporation

*Hughson, Roy V. (ed.), *Effective Communications for Engineers* (New York: McGraw-Hill, 1974), p. 106.

Figure 1.

actual sales statistics, expense forms, flow charts, area maps, chemical formulas, equipment specifications. Note that this information is usually given in the "fine print" of the text details or in the Appendix.

HOW WILL THE READER USE YOUR INFORMATION?

The answer to this third question will help you decide what details to include. Will he use the report as the basis for a decision? If so, should the facts be presented persuasively to win his cooperation?

Is the information merely to keep him informed of some advance in his field? If so, you will give a broad scope of the problem or discovery and zero in on the significance of the new information for other projects or decisions.

Will he need to duplicate or build on your work? If so, give him directions—all the ifs, ands, whats, and hows.

HOW MUCH DOES THE READER ALREADY KNOW ABOUT THE SUBJECT?

Do not spend time telling the reader what is obvious, but be sure you give him enough background on the problem so he understands the solution. Avoid jargon for those readers who are outside your narrow field.

For example, take the term "working interest." The term refers to investment interest on property, equipment, or research; a company may have "sole" or "joint" interest in a particular project. Accountants handling expenses usually use the term to mean *net* working interest—interest *after* royalties, taxes, or other specified expenses. But accountants dealing only with revenue use the term to mean *gross* working interest—interest *before* royalties, taxes, or other specified expenses.

An engineer calling the Accounting Department to find out what his company's working interest on the Upton Project is may get two different answers from two different accountants. Or more perplexing, the engineer may talk to an accountant who handles both revenue and expenses. "Do you want *net* or *gross* working interest?" the accountant asks.

"Uh . . . I don't know," the engineer may stammer. "What's the difference?"

A writer who fails to consider his audience before using such unexplained and variable terms courts misunderstanding.

And even if your audience understands all the concepts and terms you use, the audience may need more detail due to uninvolvement in the problem or project. For instance, if you have been collaborating daily by phone with your reader, you may not need to explain the particular significance of certain test results. If, however, you mentioned the significant test results only briefly two months earlier, you may need to remind him again of the significance for the decision at hand.

How much your reader knows dictates *how much* detail and *what* detail you must include in *which* sections of your report or memo. It's far better to err by giving too much detail than too little.

To sum up this step: Identify your reader or readers. Focus on the main interests of each reader or group. Decide how your audience will use your information and what your audience already knows about the subject. For an example of how this step applies to this book's contents, see Appendix A, Step One.

STEP TWO: ANTICIPATE SPECIAL PROBLEMS IN YOUR READER'S REACTIONS

From time to time in your business career, you will have to write to the reader who, despite all the facts laid before him, will habitually respond: "But I still think . . . " If you know you're dealing with such a person or group, anticipate reactions, questions, and alternatives; don't just cross your fingers and hope for the best. Plan.

WILL THERE BE SKEPTICISM?

Are you refuting existing data? Has your past work damaged your credibility? Is your product or service unusually expensive? If so, why? Will you need to convince the reader of a need or a problem?

If skepticism is involved, you'll need to document your conclusions and recommendations more heavily than you ordinarily would. Or perhaps you'll need to refute the validity of existing data or alternative solutions. You can't simply hope that the reader will overcome a skeptical attitude and give you the benefit of the doubt. You have to stamp out reservations aggressively.

IS THERE A PERSONALITY OR SITUATIONAL PROBLEM?

Will your reader have to lose face to accept your recommendations? Will he get pressure from a superior because of your message? Will you create extra work for him? Do you and the reader have a personality clash? Do you want to fire his brother-in-law?

If you uncover a personal or situational problem, you'll need to make a conscious effort to be as tactful and objective as possible. Find a way to let your reader save his dignity. If you can't, you'll need to overwhelm him with supporting evidence. If your message makes your own past decisions look incompetent, you'll need to detail why your past decisions were logical at that time, or why you were misinformed, or why the picture has changed. If you're creating extra work for someone, you'll need to impress the reader with the importance of your request or directive.

For example, consider the following situation: Every month you send out a memo to all departments requesting statistics about work in progress, statistics you will incorporate into your own report to be presented at the monthly Board of Directors meeting. Your memo reads:

> Monthly reports should be submitted to my office no later than April 14, so that my staff can prepare the final report for the Board of Directors meeting to be held April 28.

Is There a Skepticism Problem?

Perhaps you have a special problem in that many of your readers fail to submit their reports to you by the specified date—in this case, April 14. A few even hand-deliver them only a day or two before the board meeting. Their delay then causes your staff to have to work overtime to prepare the final report.

Why are these people late with their reports? Perhaps because you've included the date of the board meeting, they know that they have a "grace" period, the time you've allowed yourself to prepare the final report. By anticipating this special procrastination problem, you could omit the board meeting date in your memo, thereby eliminating the "double due date" effect.

Of course, you can never be sure you have erased all skepticism or dismissed all personal or situational problems, but be aware that such problems exist, and attempt to handle them from the outset. For an example of how this step applies to this book, see Appendix A, Step Two.

STEP THREE: OUTLINE YOUR MESSAGE FUNCTIONALLY

We have two kinds of drivers in the world: those who look at a map before they leave home and those who "drive until they find it." Similarly, we have two kinds of writers: those who plan what they want to say before they write and those who write while they decide. If given a choice, most readers will try to avoid the latter.

But to the writer, the word "outline" often brings to mind the drudgery of high school or college English courses, where outlines had to be in parallel form—either all sentences or all topics, never mixed. If the first word in Point A was an adjective, Points B, C, D, and E had to begin with an adjective. If Point II had an "A," it also had to have a "B."

Let me state from the outset that I advocate *functional* outlining, not the rigors just mentioned. Topic sentence outlines can help you remember exactly where you are going with each point.

But if the details in the paragraphs can be summed up in a topic phrase on your outline, that's functional. The outlining process should be as short or as long as necessary for you to turn out a well-organized report, letter, or memo.

For this 133-page book, I worked from a four-page, double-spaced outline. For another book of the same length, I worked from a twenty-page outline. You need to outline as much or as little as necessary to keep to the narrow path.

But outline, you must! And yes, although my outline may be only five words, I outline even a short letter.

Someone has aptly questioned: "If you don't have time to do it right the first time, how will you ever find time to do it over?" That observation was never more appropriate than for the task of writing. Working without an outline almost always assures a rewrite or time on the phone "interpreting."

First, outlining organizes your message. Outlining lets you see logical relationships and visualize major and minor ideas.

Second, outlining speeds up the first draft. The hardest part of writing is beginning. It's the fish thing again—catching hold of the assignment without getting finned. Once you have summarized the main points in sentences or phrases in an outline with details to support each idea, half the work is done. Your first draft is simply a matter of filling in the flesh around the skeleton.

Third, outlining helps you condense the final draft. An outline makes you focus on the central message without spending words "working into" each new topic:

Dear Mr. Borwin:

This letter will acknowledge receipt of your July 9 letter in which you requested information concerning the status of the Veta project with regard to the feasibility of establishing a new plant in . . .

Instead, with an outline you already know where you're going, and you can begin with the important message:

Dear Mr. Borwin:

I have decided to proceed immediately with the Veta project. . . .

Fourth, outlining eliminates major revisions in the editing step. Without a plan, you often have to do a cut-and-paste job of editing, moving page 4 to the middle of page 2. Then that move calls for a new transitional sentence to keep the logical flow of ideas and a new paragraph conclusion to bridge the gap to the following idea. Getting the order right the first time precludes later major revisions.

Finally, outlining helps you keep your sanity and train of thought through interruptions. No matter how many phone calls, appointments, drop-ins, or holidays interrupt your writing task, an outline will show you where you've been and where you're headed.

Five good reasons to outline—remember them when you're tempted to skip this step to "save time."

ARRANGE INTO BASIC FORMAT FOR REPORTS, LETTERS, AND MEMOS

The traditional report, letter, or memo follows the format in Figure 2, varying slightly from company to company.

TRADITIONAL REPORT FORMAT (ascending order)

I. Summary	(overview of entire report)	
II. Body	(introduction—history, problem, scope)	
	(discussion—methods, details)	
	(conclusions and recommendations—test results, suggested actions)	
III. Appendixes	(optional evidence—tables, maps, charts, forms, questionnaires, etc.)	

Figure 2. Items of most interest to your reader are buried.

The problem with this traditional ascending format is that the items of major interest to the most important audience—management—are buried in the last sections of the report. And as you noticed from the Westinghouse Electric Corporation study on how managers read reports (Figure 1), that's where the reader has to dig out what he really wants to know.

Understanding a message written in this ascending format is an uphill climb (see Figure 3). The details gradually unfold as the reader trudges toward the top of the hill: the message.

If you organize your report or letter or memo in the traditional order, you have failed to consider your audience's point of view: Instead, you have written the report from *your* point of view. Why you started the study, what you found out had already been done in related fields, how you computed figures, and what results you finally discovered. For the most part, the management reader is not interested in your trouble, but rather in your conclusions and recommendations.

A second reason for giving the reader the conclusions first is to increase his comprehension. Reading experts have done study after study on which to base their advice that the reader should skim a report's or book's headings, illustrations, and summary sections before reading for details. Different experts may call this "previewing" or "prereading" the material, but the effect on comprehension is the same: When the reader knows from the beginning where he's going, he can better understand and remember the details.

Certainly, the ascending structure has a use—for novels, jokes, and anecdotes. In these, the writer sets the atmosphere, gives background, and creates suspense to whet the appetite for the punch line.

Even for an occasional report, the ascending order may be used when you think the conclusions or recommendations are going to displease the reader. You paint the picture slowly and hope the evidence along the way will convince the reader to adopt your conclusions by the time you get around to stating them. But even here, the ascending order is dangerous. By the time the reader gets to your conclusions, he may have reached different conclu-

Ascending Outline

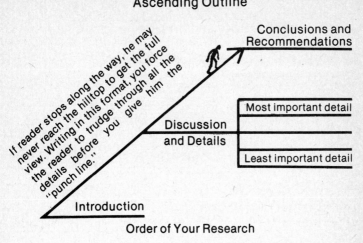

If reader stops along the way, he may never reach the hilltop to get the full view. Writing in this format, you force the reader to trudge through all the details before you give him the "punch line."

Conclusions and Recommendations

Most important detail

Discussion and Details

Least important detail

Introduction

Order of Your Research

Descending Outline

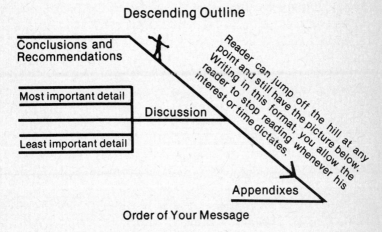

Conclusions and Recommendations

Most important detail

Discussion

Least important detail

Reader can jump off the hill at any point and still have the picture below. Writing in this format, you allow the reader to stop reading whenever his interest or time dictates.

Appendixes

Order of Your Message

Figure 3.

sions or have a strong case built against your interpretations all along the way.

For the most part, business writing should be straightforward, not suspenseful: What's the message? What action next? Who, when, where, why, how details? Optional evidence? To see how this format applies to this book, see Appendix A, Step Three.

FUNCTIONAL REPORT, LETTER, OR MEMO FORMAT

(Descending Order)

What's the message? (conclusions)	Narrow angle to fit audience
What action next? (recommendations)	What action do you plan to take? Or what action do you want the reader to take?
Who, when, where, why, how details? (discussion)	Not all should be included in every report. Which details are important to your audience?
Optional evidence? (Appendixes)	Tables, charts, maps, graphs, forms, questionnaires, copies of past correspondence, etc.

Figure 4.

WHAT'S THE MESSAGE?

Begin your report, letter, or memo with the answer to the most important question: We should open a new plant in Houston. We should expand the Atlanta warehouse. We have perfected a new excavation tool that will be 20 percent more economical than what we're now using. Your operators don't know how to monitor such-and-such machine. Your year-end reports contain two discrepancies. We held a pre-award meeting with the vendor and are hesitant to sign his contract.

You expect this same summary daily in informal conversation. For example, you arrive home late at night after a hard day's work and you're ready to shower and relax. You ask your spouse:

"What about the shower leak?"

"Well, I thought I'd never get a plumber out here because there's been an emergency situation in the northeast part of town and—"

"Is it fixed?" you cut in.

"Yes. After a real hassle. First, he—"

"How much?" you interrupt again.

"Seventy-eight dollars."

You roll your eyes upward and head for a towel. Now that you have the most important message you're willing to listen to all the who, when, why, and how details.

Do the same for your reader: Give him what he wants to know at the beginning, and do so briefly. If you can't summarize your "bottom line" message for most reports, letters, or memos in about two or three sentences, you don't have the focus narrow enough.

With the message up front, your reader can pay attention to your details with enlightened purpose.

WHAT ACTION NEXT?

Based on that narrowly focused message, fill in the second division of the basic format. What is your reader supposed to do about your message? Should he assign someone to begin a new project? Should he buy the land? Should he discontinue testing the system? Should he modify his computer program? Should he turn the case over to the Legal Department? Should he refund your money and send shipping instructions to return the damaged merchandise?

When your reader knows what action you want him to take, he can listen more intelligently to the details about how to do it.

Or perhaps you need to take the next action, and you merely want to inform your reader of your plans: Will you begin a survey of all employees about their options and needs in training? Will you assign someone else in your department to follow up your present study? Will you write a contract with a new service company? Will you fire an accountant who has continually refused to work overtime? Will you send another progress report in two months?

Again, if your reader first knows what you plan to do, he can read the details about your action more intelligently.

WHO, WHEN, WHERE, WHY, HOW DETAILS?

Give necessary details; omit the obvious. Usually the "why" and the "how" will be the essential details of your message. Why have you discarded the old policy? How will you put the new policy into effect? Why have you hesitated in awarding the contract? How will you solicit new bids before the construction deadline? Why did this equipment become obsolete so soon after purchase? How do you propose to avoid this obsolescence in future purchases?

Of course, other of these details must be answered when the answers are not obvious to your reader: When will you require employees to begin using the new ID badge? Where will the new spray be most successful? Who will oversee the machine's marketing? Who will arrange for advertising the new consulting service? How are the questionnaires to be distributed and collected?

The "who," "when," and "where" details are generally already contained in the message or action sentences at the beginning of your report. If they have not been mentioned, however, elaborate on such details, as necessary, in the third section.

Remember that any obvious details should be omitted. For example, if you want to save money for the company, you don't need to explain why. Such unnecessary details merely add length. On the other hand, if your targeted audience will not understand the implication of the changes you're requesting or will be skeptical that such changes are necessary, you may need to elaborate extensively on "why."

OPTIONAL EVIDENCE?

Finally, you will select and place in the Appendix (or attach to a memo or letter) any optional material you need to support your conclusions, recommendations, and discussion details.

Contrast this functional report, letter, or memo format arranged in descending order to the traditional report format arranged in ascending order in Figure 5. This expansion outlines a service problem report written to a client who has had equipment failure. In the ascending-order outline notice the buried message of prime interest to the most important readers, management. But in the descending-order outline the message comes at the beginning of the report. From reading the first section, the manager

ASCENDING OUTLINE

I. Introduction
  A. Past equipment failures
  B. Present couplings failure
II. Methods
  A. Metallurgical analysis
  B. Torque-turn analysis
  C. Field investigation
III. Discussion
  A. Metallurgical analysis
    1. Hardness results
    2. Iron sulfide
  B. Torque-turn analysis
    1. Bottom turns incorrectly monitored
    2. Incorrect torque setting
  C. Field investigations
IV. Conclusions and Recommendations
  A. Conclusions
    1. Causes of failed couplings
    2. Torque-turn unit not calibrated
  B. Recommendations
    1. Investigate causes of embrittlement
    2. Pinpoint hydrogen leak
V. Appendixes

DESCENDING OUTLINE

I. Conclusions and Recommendations
  A. Conclusions
    1. Causes of failed couplings
    2. Torque-turn unit not calibrated
  B. Recommendations
    1. Investigate causes of embrittlement
    2. Pinpoint hydrogen leak
II. Methods and Findings
  A. Metallurgical analysis
    1. Hardness results
    2. Iron sulfide
  B. Torque-turn analysis
    1. Bottom turns incorrectly monitored
    2. Incorrect torque setting
  C. Field investigations
III. Appendixes

Figure 5. Ascending/descending expanded outline.

has a "photo" of the entire report findings. He can stop reading anywhere along the way that time or interest dictates and get on with the necessary repairs to his equipment.

The second section of the outline (the "why" and the "how" details) adds to his understanding of how the writer arrived at his conclusions and recommendations about the equipment failure.

The third section of the outline (the Appendixes) is for the manager who wants more evidence and discussion of the details and for the specialist who will actually correct the problem by pinpointing the hydrogen leak.

Notice that in the descending-order outline the introduction is missing. Frequently, most material in introductions is already known and/or boring. Any necessary background material can be woven into the discussion section as explanation in the "why" and the "how" of your message.

Contrast the same two arrangements in the traditional and functional memos in Figure 6.

Remember, business reading is done on the run. Billboard advertisers know this; brochure designers know this; even your kids know this when they leave a note on the kitchen table, "Please leave me five dollars for school—will explain later."

Business readers demand that you get to the point—the bottom line.

The format for directive memos varies slightly from the above-suggested arrangement in that "the message" *is* the action; these two segments become a single item. And often a directive memo should begin with the answer to "why." Winning employees' cooperation is much easier if you state a reason for the directive.

Walk into a colleague's office in the middle of the afternoon and announce that he needs to evacuate the building immediately. "Why?" is almost an automatic response. On the other hand, walk in and announce that there's been a bomb threat and that he needs to evacuate immediately. He'll beat you through the doorway.

If you're going to ask employees to go through the trouble of filling out new insurance forms, explain that you are changing insurance companies because past claims have not been paid promptly and that you want your employees to be reimbursed fully for their expenses as soon as possible. A plausible reason makes almost any directive less arbitrary.

TRADITIONAL MEMO

DETAILS — The reader is thinking, "So what?"

XYZ depreciates general properties on an annual rate of 10 percent. Most of the computer equipment is basically in this general properties category. An exception to this depreciation schedule is some of our video-type Lexitrons, depreciated at a 20 percent rate.

ACTION — Reader is thinking, "why now?"

MESSAGE — The reader finally gets the point

I suggest that we review our 10 percent rate for the depreciation of this equipment. We are in the process of purchasing some major items for the word-processing area and the technology in this field changes rapidly and could affect the market value of the equipment drastically.

If you agree with this review, sign and return this memo to me.

FUNCTIONAL MEMO

MESSAGE

ACTION and why detail

We are in the process of purchasing some major items for the word-processing area. I suggest that we review our 10 percent rate for depreciation of this type of equipment because rapid technological advances in this field could affect the market value of our equipment drastically.

other details to justify the action

XYZ typically depreciates general properties on an annual rate of 10 percent, and most of our computer equipment is basically in this general property category. An exception to this depreciation schedule is some of our video-type Lexitrons, depreciated at 20 percent.

If you agree with this review, sign and return this memo to me.

Figure 6. Traditional vs. functional format for reports, letters, and memos.

DIRECTIVE MEMO FORMAT

Why the message?	(This is a short phrase or statement to smooth the way for the directive.)
What's the message?	(The message is the action you expect.)
Who, when, where, why, how details?	(Give all details the reader needs to take the action.)
Optional evidence?	(Can you include an example to show him how to take the action?)

Figure 7.

Consider the following unorganized directive memo:

To: All Company Employees
Subject: Copy Machine Use
A list of civic organizations for which the management has approved use of the company copy machines is posted in Room 202. It has long been company policy to extend our services cordially to such activities and organizations. However, in the past months there has been a rash of nonbusiness use of our copiers, which has overextended our budget allocations for copying. It is important that we watch future expenses closely. It is the responsibility of everyone to utilize stationery supplies and copiers for company or especially approved businesses.

When an employee reads this memo, he has to wade through the first three sentences (two thirds of the memo) to get to anything that interests him. The author has violated the first rule of writing: Consider the interests of the reader. While reading the first few sentences, the employee is wondering, "So what?" What does this have to do with me?" Then when he gets to the point—that you want to restrict personal use of the copier—he still doesn't know to what extent. Does the "especially approved businesses" at the end of the memo refer to the already approved civic uses mentioned earlier in the memo? Or can he ask you to "especially approve" other copying for him when the need arises? In the writer's mind, he has probably connected those two details, but the reader will not necessarily go back and make that same connection.

If you write such a disorganized memo, you'll find yourself doing several follow-ups to get the point across—as the writer of the above memo admitted he had had to do. Compare the above disorganized memo to the following one arranged in the basic directive memo format:

> To: All Company Employees
> Subject: Personal Use of the Copier
> To stay within our budget allocations for copying, I am asking that all employees limit nonbusiness copying to approved civic activities. If you are in doubt about which activities are approved, please check the list posted on the bulletin board, Room 202.

Notice that this version is shorter but leaves no doubt about what action (or nonaction in this case) you are requesting. Organization always aids clarity.

After you become familiar with this basic functional format (What's the message? What action next? Who, when, where, why, and how details? Optional evidence?), you can organize most simple reports, letters, or memos in your head. Rarely will major revisions be necessary.

EXPAND THE BASIC FORMAT

When your report message is complex, you will need to expand the basic format into a more detailed outline to accommodate complicated and numerous details.

BEGIN WITH A RANDOM LIST

If you want to include three details in a memo or letter, you have a choice of six ways to arrange those three details. If you have four details to include, you can choose from twenty-four combinations. The reason many writers stare at a blank page trying to decide how to begin is that they are trying to visualize all the possible combinations of major ideas or details and choose the best arrangement. To examine mentally all the possible combinations of even three or four details (without seeing something on paper) is virtually impossible.

Skip the staring stage and begin with a random list of ideas as they come to mind. Don't be concerned with what should come first, second, third, and so forth, or which points are major ideas and which are minor ones.

Figure 8 shows a random list of ideas to be incorporated into a report on alleviating the overcrowded company library by installing movable shelves and converting paper records to microfilm. Notice that some items on the list are in sentence form, others in words or sentences. Generally, when sentences come to mind, you should write down the entire thought, because a complete statement gives the complete focus of your idea.

If you list only "New York sales," when you get ready to write the corresponding paragraph you may have forgotten what you were going to say about New York sales. If instead you write "Compare New York sales to Boston sales," you'll remember immediately where you are headed with the paragraph. You'll avoid "working into" your message with wasted words, which will need to be cut in the editing stage. Of course, if sentences don't materialize as you're making the random list, just jot down the phrase or word and proceed.

In the random listing, also be sure to add all the details, illustrations, or figures that come to mind. Everything you put down in the outline will save you time later.

Even for a letter, a random list is a good idea if you have several details to include (see Figure 9). Note in Figure 9 the lettering beside the numbers—2a and 4a. Such notations remind the writer to link those two ideas together in the same sentence.

For an example of random listing for this book, see Appendix B.

ARRANGE THE RANDOM LIST IN LOGICAL ORDER

After finishing the random list, you can see relationships in your ideas and details. Now is the time to rearrange these items in logical order, as illustrated in Figure 10. Also, at this point you may decide that some items on the list should be dropped altogether.

If you are describing a process, you will probably shuffle ideas

REPON ON OVERCROWDED LIBRARY

Present space problem —
- too many unread magazines
- boxes in aisles — too narrow walkways
- inconvenient checkout

Leasing more space in XYZ Bldg. — too expensive
traveling problem between locations

Renting more space in warehouse is short-term solution

Cost of microfilming — favorable

Space savings with microfilming

Movable shelves — extra aisle space
— increased shelf capacity by 66%

Many paper records could be destroyed

Clerk salary for microfilming section — salary
— pkg. of benefits

Remodeling costs — new carpet
— new checkout counter
— new dividers on east end

What records to film first

Misfiling — minimal with microfilm
— duplicates at a nominal cost
— easier to handle than paper records

Location of movable shelves (include drawings of present
and proposed arrangements)

Quarterly, semi-annual, and annual reports to be filmed first

Figure 8. Begin with a random list.

into chronological order. If you are evaluating two vendor contracts, you may shuffle ideas into a point-by-point comparison. If you are persuading management to move a warehouse, you may arrange your arguments from the weakest to the strongest.

Some ideas will lend themselves to more than one logical arrangement. For example, let's say you are writing a vendor about your dissatisfaction with a word processor. You might arrange the letter chronologically: dates and description of problems as they developed, dates of unanswered or delayed service calls, dates and details about phone calls to ask questions about the machine's capabilities.

③ Many accounts in primary market category.
④ Contact key persons.
⑤ Forward names of interested accounts to Don Doe.
② Primary markets — small hospitals, clinics.
① Theophylline — now on market.
⑥ Send copy of "leads" to me.
⑦ Questions about Theophylline — Don Doe.
⑦a Contact group practices with pediatricians or allergists.
④a Tell key persons about procedure for Theophylline and monitoring blood levels.

Figure 9. Random list for letters. Numbering beside the details indicates sequence for details in final form. Note that the format is still: message first (1, 2, 2a, 3); action next (4, 4a); finally, the details (5, 6, 7).

Or you could arrange the details in order of significance of the problems: machine features that do not accomplish your objectives, two ignored service requests, one delayed service call, rudeness of maintenance personnel.

Or you could arrange the details of your dissatisfaction by category: features you need but that the machine can't perform; features the machine has but that you do not need; costs of initial purchase, maintenance, and supplies; overall appearance, such as bulkiness and unsightly cables strung over the office.

Investigate several logical arrangements and choose the most appropriate one for your purposes.

The following guidelines offer extra help in frequently used logical arrangements:

Instructions

(Policy manuals, user manuals, department procedures, investigative procedures, etc.)

1. Explain reasons for change in old method, if cooperation is a problem.
2. List materials, forms, or equipment needed.
3. Mention any safety precautions and repeat again before the step in which the precaution should be taken.

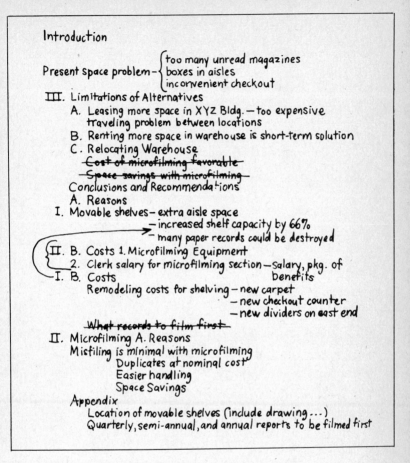

Figure 10. Random List to Logical Order.

4. Give steps in chronological order and indicate each step in a separate sentence.
5. Write sentences in the imperative mood. ("Monitor these machines for . . . ," not "These machines should be monitored for . . .")
6. Give examples when possible and place supporting tables, drawings, or illustrations as close to each step as possible.

Process

(Investigative research, progress reports, etc.)
1. Overview the objectives of the process or project.
2. Pinpoint and mention the number of stages involved.
3. Explain any equipment, materials, or terms the reader will not understand in the details to follow. (Details to be covered here depend on what you discovered when you "considered your audience.")
4. Explain the process chronologically.

Definition or Description

(Job descriptions, project overviews, equipment or service brochures, etc.)
1. Overview the object's or person's function.
2. Describe equipment's appearance or organizational structure, if necessary. In describing equipment, begin with internal parts and move to the outer. In describing an organization, begin from the bottom up or from the top down.
3. Describe the operation in detail.

Question/Answer

(Analysis of data, ideas, attitudes, policies, etc.)
1. Pose unknowns or problems.
2. State your hypothesis or answer.
3. Present your support in descending order of significance in most presentations.
4. Address and refute any alternative hypotheses or answers.
5. Restate your answer or hypothesis.

Persuasive

(Proposals, sales brochures, etc.)
1. State your conclusion.
2. If you are sure the reader will read the entire document, present support in ascending order of significance. Begin with the least evidence and build your case to the strongest, unrefutable evidence. (The inherent danger here always is that your reader may stop reading before he gets to your strongest evidence.)

3. Include cost analysis.
4. Refute objections and address alternatives.
5. Restate your major evidence and conclusion.

Comparison/Contrast

(Of contracts, services, equipment, performances, plans of action, etc.)

1. State the conclusion—two things are primarily alike or different; either both will serve equally well and meet your requirements, or one is superior to the other.

   (*Caution*: If you intend to concentrate on one side—either similarities or differences—presenting both sides dilutes your main point. If the major angle is "differences," lump all the exceptions—similarities—into one "exception" paragraph or section.)

2. Present the predominant conclusions in a point-by-point analysis in descending order of significance.

3. Restate your conclusion.

In some report writing, of course, you will combine several of these formats and guidelines. Choose any logical arrangement that fits your material and your reader's purpose; that arrangement should be evident as you look over your random list and see relationships among major and minor ideas.

If the body of your report does not fall into place naturally, the chances are that you have the wrong method of arrangement. Rearranging and shuffling your outline into a different order is much easier and quicker than rearranging an entire draft.

For an expanded outline of what is contained in this book, see the Contents page.

No matter which order you choose for the expanded outline, the basic format structure should remain the same: What's the message (conclusions)? What action next (recommendations)? Who, when, where, why, and how details (body or discussion, containing the bulk of your expanded outline)? Optional evidence (Appendix or other attachments)?

Most letters, too, including "transmittal" letters, should be arranged the same as the informational memos or reports mentioned above. But consider the following guidelines when writing letters with a built-in "special problem":

Letter Requesting Action

1. As with the directive memo, briefly pave the way for your request.
2. Center on one action you want the reader to take. Don't make your request a by-the-way item in the final paragraph.
3. Give your reader details to take the action.
4. Supply an incentive if possible—promise goodwill or recall other values for the reader.

The following letter requesting action will likely meet a responsive audience:

Dear Ms. Syden:

The recent closing of your account is of special concern to us. We are interested in the reason behind your decision and your suggestions as to how we might improve our services.

Would you please help us by answering a few questions on the enclosed form? Any additional comments you may have would be very much welcomed. Do not feel that you must sign this form.

The enclosed stamped envelope is for your convenience.

It is always a pleasure serving you and we only hope to serve you better in the future. Again, thank you for any help you may give us in completing the enclosed form.

What makes this letter effective, even to an angry client who has closed her account? First, the opening paragraph sounds like the writer has the reader's interest in mind. And, of course, anyone likes to have someone ask for his opinion or advice.

Second, the desired action is central to the message, not a by-the-way matter in the closing paragraph, and the writer has made it easy for the reader to give her opinion. You'll note also that the writer doesn't assume his reader will respond; the last statement says, "Again, thank you for any help you *may* give us in completing the enclosed form."

Finally, the writer offers incentive—improved service to the customer should she ever reconsider doing business with their company again.

Negative Response to a Request

1. Begin with a positive note, something the reader can feel good about.
2. Build up with reasons for the negative response. (Use inductive development here because the tone is especially important.)
3. Put the negative as positively as possible. (Position is important. Place the negative in the internal part of the paragraph.)
4. End with an unrelated goodwill statement.

The following "no, thank you" letter leaves a pleasant taste in the reader's mouth:

Dear Mr. Brown:

We received your announcement of the seminar "Managing Your Inventory"; this subject is of particular interest to many in the petroleum industry. However, our purchasing is handled by each supervisor at the project site because needs differ from one facility to the other. Therefore, our staff here will be unable to take advantage of your presentation.

Please contact us again about other presentations; we would be particularly interested in a workshop which considered some of the same topics as your executive seminar of May 15.

Best wishes for your continued success.

The writer begins with a compliment that the seminar presenter has chosen an interesting topic to many in the industry, then follows with a specific reason his staff will be unable to "take advantage" of the presentation. By the time the reader gets to the last sentence of the first paragraph, he already knows he's going to get a "no" but doesn't feel a personal put-down. And the closing statement is not only positive but also flattering. Who doesn't like to be considered a success?

The third kind of "special problem" letter involves a complaint. Some consider this the easiest kind of letter to write, especially when the error or problem has nothing to do with their own ineptness and when they share no portion of the blame. A complaint letter, however, is probably the most difficult letter to compose when the objective is to get a problem corrected and to leave a good relationship intact.

Complaint Letter

1. Give all pertinent information about the problem or error, but be brief.
2. State exactly what you are asking the reader to do.
3. Be confident in tone, not sarcastic or aggressive.

Which of the two letters below would you be more likely to respond to if you were Mr. Smith?

Dear Mr. Smith:

With our letter of November 13, under Release No. 13 of the subject order, we requested you to furnish five perma-stamp items. The requirements were explicitly detailed.

On January 11 we received four of the required stamps—eight weeks after the order. Of these four, three were specified to be deluxe mount; all four were furnished as spring mount! We were advised that the fifth stamp was back-ordered, even though this particular stamp was one of your *stock* stamps, No. ST-844. Now today, ten weeks from our order date, we have received this stock stamp. And this stamp as supplied is *not* in accordance with your catalog illustration.

Mr. Smith, we are extremely disappointed over the Zurich performance in this matter. You have ignored our specifications and shipping orders and ignored your own catalog descriptions! Since this is not the first time we have experienced problems with the manner in which our requirements are serviced, we have to question seriously the desirability of continuing to purchase your product. In view of this, I thought I ought to call your attention to these facts.

Or:

Dear Mr. Smith,

In our letter of November 13, under Release No. 13 of the subject order, we requested five perma-stamp items; this order has not been filled to our satisfaction.

On January 11 (eight weeks after our order) we received four of the five stamps. Three of these four stamps were spring mount rather than the deluxe mount, as specified in our order.

We were advised at that time that the fifth stamp was back-ordered, even though this is one of your stock stamps, No. ST-844.

The fifth stamp finally arrived today (ten weeks after our order date), and it does not match your catalog illustration.

Therefore, I am returning the three spring-mount stamps and keeping the one deluxe-mount stamp that we can use. Do not send the other three deluxe-mount stamps as previously ordered, because we have had to purchase those locally for immediate use. I am also returning the fifth back-ordered stamp, No. ST-844, because we specifically need the features pictured in your catalog.

Please send a corrected bill for the one deluxe-mount stamp, allowing reimbursement for our shipping charges in returning the incorrectly sent merchandise.

Thank you for your prompt attention in correcting this order.

If you would more likely respond to the second, I'm with you. The major weakness in the first letter is that Mr. Smith has no idea how the customer expects the problem to be corrected: Does he want to keep the substituted stamp? Should the company send on the delayed deluxe-mount stamps? Does he want a refund on everything?

The second weakness, of course, in the first letter is the tone. Word and phrases like "explicitly detailed," "extremely disappointed," and "ignored" make the reader feel like an incompetent person (he may well be, but you'll likely not motivate him to be competent with such word choices). And did you hear the writer shouting with the italicized words and the vehement punctuation marks? The threat toward the end of the letter leaves the reader ready to call the bluff, and either way the cards fall, he'll probably not be too disappointed.

Again, writing a complaint letter simply to complain is one thing; but when you're writing to get corrective action, get specific about the problem and the solution and show a positive, confident attitude that your reader will see things as you do.

When the situation is reversed, write your apology letter with the following guidelines in mind:

Apology Letter

1. Focus immediately on positive action (not just words) taken to rectify the situation rather than recalling the details of the damage or problem.

2. Briefly, in a positive way, explain how the mistake happened.
3. Assure the reader that you will take precaution against future errors.
4. Make the reader feel that you are truly sorry about the problem and that you value his goodwill or business.

The following letter is a response to an upset insurance client who had filed a theft claim and found her coverage inadequate to allow her to replace the stolen items. In her complaint letter she blames the insurance company for not talking with her about adding coverage with past renewals.

Dear Ms. Bowden:

We have enclosed the new appraisal schedule for jewelry to be covered in your renewal policy. I'm sorry our representative did not bring the need for reappraisal to your attention earlier; a new agent has assumed responsibility for your account and is still learning the ins and outs of the insurance business.

If you have other items that may need to be reappraised such as cameras, china, silver, furs, coins, or fine arts, we'd be happy to come out again and work with you in providing adequate coverage.

If the increased coverage outlined in the attachment is satisfactory, please sign and return the appraisal to our office.

We're making a note in your file to review annually your appraisals so that you will be fully protected in case of future loss.

Thank you for the opportunity to provide this coverage.

The writer sounds apologetic and concerned even though he is not entirely to blame for the lack of coverage. He has apologized with action (the reappraisal schedule) and a reason for the oversight. Notice that the says he will take precaution against future losses, but wisely he does not state that the client never will be underinsured again. Claims of future perfection convince few people and disappoint many. Customers often forgive the biblical seventy times seven when you throw yourself on their mercy, but expectations run high for saints.

Again, note that all these "special problem" letters contain the basic format information. The difference is that such letters require rearranging, highlighting, and soothing to accommodate special reactions you anticipate from your reader.

REVIEW YOUR OUTLINE

Have you stayed with the single angle all the way through? Have you dealt with special problems you identified in Step Two? Have you refuted skepticism and alternative suggestions? Is your message presented in descending order—the conclusions and recommendations up front, the discussion and details following? Have you gone off on tangents that have no bearing on your main focus? (If so, delete that idea from your outline and don't waste time writing the paragraph that later will have to be cut.) What examples or supplementary material could you attach to make the message more complete or easily understood?

Check with your supervisor about your writing plan. A professional writer rarely considers writing a complete article or book without a prior go-ahead from an editor. When a magazine writer gets an idea for an article, he ferrets out an unusual angle and then does a brief outline to send to an editor for approval. If the editor answers "Sounds great," the writer can prepare his manuscript with confidence that he'll make a sale. The editor may respond, however, that the writer's angle doesn't fit the magazine's readership and that the writer should try a new angle. Or he may respond, "I like your angle, but leave out the part about the mushrooms in Gawangatan." In either case, the writer has profited. If the beginning angle was wrong, he has saved himself a major revision or a flat turndown.

Your time is no less valuable. You should check with all supervisors or peers who will have to agree on or approve your final report or letter. Make sure they agree with your interpretations of the data and your conclusions and recommendations. They may also point out skepticism or other special problems they foresee down the line—problems you should deal with the first time around.

You may find that setting up a conference is a convenient way to get feedback from those who must agree or approve. But if this isn't possible, furnish each person with a copy of your outline and get individual comments and approval.

Prewriting approval provides peace of mind. Writing a first draft is much easier when you know that you'll not be rewriting a report from a completely new perspective.

STEP FOUR: DEVELOP THE FIRST DRAFT

By the time you reach this step, half your work is finished. Developing the first draft should go quickly and smoothly if you have followed the preceding planning steps.

COLLECT AND ASSEMBLE DATA

Assemble your data from published research, interviews, letters, experience, observations, or tests. If some of your research is hard to handle because of odd physical size, note a summary of the available data on an index card and add the card to the pile. This "reminder" card will help you remember to relocate the oversized flow chart when you're ready to write that particular section of the report.

Next, label each card as to subject matter in the upper *left-hand* corner. Use short, informative labels such as "Stress analysis test results" or "Reasons for low mercury levels."

Now, with an eye to your outline, label in the upper *right-hand* corner each notecard or graph with a corresponding outline number (see Figure 11).

During this labeling step, you may uncover major weaknesses in your previous research. If your primary point is that a piece of equipment is too expensive, you may discover that you have little support for that opinion. In that case, you should postpone writing until you've collected more supporting information—perhaps statistics on costs of all other alternative equipment.

On the other hand, while matching data to your outline, you may discover that you have unnecessary information. Avoid the temptation to include all the extra data simply because it represents time-consuming work. (In the process of developing a new water supply system, you may have discovered three other plans that didn't work!) Spare your reader all the details of your

---

III.
B.

Overloaded shelving

"Floor-load studies have been invaluable in modern library designs. The present study showed 300 lbs. per square foot. . . ."

Figure 11. Notecard notations.

failures and side adventures. Such irrelevant material damages the thrust of your overall report.

After collecting, labeling, and matching your data to your outline, sort the cards into piles. A long conference tables is ideal; the floor will do. Pick up one pile of data cards at a time, arrange in final order corresponding to your outline, keep the outline in front of you, and you're ready to compose the first draft.

DICTATE OR TYPE

Dictating the first draft or composing it on a typewriter takes much less time than writing it in longhand. Second, dictating produces a conversational style, not stilted prose that makes for fog. Third, when dictating, you don't fall in love with your words. Words written in longhand quickly become permanent in your mind as well as on the paper.

At first dictating may prove awkward, but with practice you will quickly improve and save yourself valuable time. Your typist will appreciate your studying the rules in Figure 12. A good expanded outline helps you move from point to point without pause. Don't worry that your sentences will not be polished; you can always correct grammatical errors or sentence structure in the editing step.

Dictating does have a drawback, however, in that it's more difficult to review dictated material than written material. If this is a problem to you, composing on a typewriter, almost as fast, may be your best alternative.

With the first draft, three fourths of your writing project is finished.

DICTATOR RULES IN THE OFFICE

Rule 1: Speak clearly and slowly. Don't mumble.

Rule 2: Give document information.
   a. Is it a letter, memo, report, rough draft, other?
   b. Paper (letterhead, bond, etc.)?
   c. Number of copies and to whom?

Rule 3: Help with spelling.
(Spell all names, streets, cities, unfamiliar terms the first few times you use them.)

Rule 4: Give specific format.
   a. Tell which titles should be centered, which should be at left margin, which should be in caps, which should be lowercase, which should be underlined.
   b. Tell where to double-space, single-space, triple space.
   c. Specify new paragraphs.
   d. Specify the manner in which you are dictating tables, etc. Say: "Set up four column headings as follows: _____, _____, _____, _____. From left to right, fill in the columns with these numbers. . . ."

Rule 5: Specify punctuation.
("Comma," "open quotes," "close quotes," "open parenthesis," "close parenthesis," etc. A secretary many times cannot tell where the punctuation marks go until you have finished the sentence; then it's too late.)

Figure 12. Dictating or typing speeds the first-draft process.

STEP FIVE: EDIT FOR CONTENT, GRAMMAR, CLARITY, CONCISENESS, AND STYLE

Editing is to a report or letter what polish is to boots. Much business writing fails because this final step is hurried or nonexistent, especially when the writing project has been short and relatively simple. And some writers confuse editing with proofreading, which is merely checking for typographical and

DICTATE—DON'T LET WORDS GROW ON YOU

grammatical errors. Editing, although it includes such errors, involves attention to much broader flaws.

Because the major work is over and you have an almost-finished product in your hands, editing can be the most rewarding and enjoyable step in the entire writing process.

Always allow a cooling-off period before beginning to edit; for a letter or memo, at least a few hours, and for a report, preferably a couple of days. Your time-management skills come into play here. When you are planning your work schedule, plan with this cooling-off period in mind. Take up a new project in the interval, then come back to editing the first report. This lets you approach your earlier work with more objectivity to catch inconsistencies not apparent when working with fresh material.

As you edit, use the standard editing symbols shown in Figure 13. If both you and your secretary use them, you can eliminate much miscommunication in this editing process.

EDIT FOR CONTENT

IS THE ANGLE NARROW AND CONSISTENT?

Any writer's first interests are usually self-interests. But remember that the first step in writing must be to consider the interests, experience, and knowledge of your reader. If his interest is money, did you sidetrack to tell him about the prestige involved in owning the new product? If he's primarily interested in speed, don't let the body of your report trail off onto the economics of the new system you're proposing. And even when you are addressing his interests, have you told him too much of what he already knows? Move the "extra" information to the Appendix or eliminate it altogether.

DOES PROPORTION MATCH EMPHASIS?

Proportion suggests importance and emphasis. Have you spent a large portion of the space justifying a minor action? Have you spent too many words telling your reader *why* you did something and too few words explaining *what* you did?

Graphs, charts, and tables can make your report look out of proportion. A good rule of thumb for their placement: If the figures are necessary for the discussion at hand, include them in the body of the report as near the text reference as possible. If they are merely evidence or optional material that you can summarize in the text, put them in the Appendix. Note the placement of figures and lists in this book's text and Appendix. Their placement tells you which I consider necessary to understanding the text and which are supplementary items.

To sum up: Make sure the proportion of the text devoted to a particular idea matches the importance of that idea.

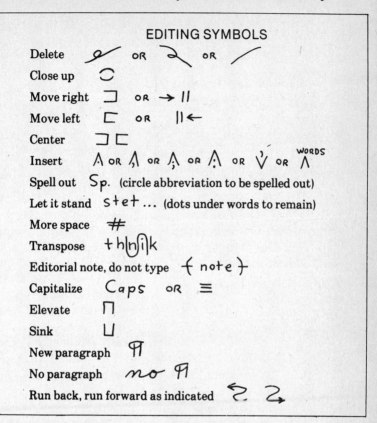

Figure 13. Consistent editing symbols add clarity and save time.

CHECK ACCURACY AND COMPLETENESS; ADD AUTHORITY

Recheck all graphs, tables, and figures. If a reader finds one error, he will often doubt everything you said in the report. One workshop participant related that he had investigated a job-related injury and wrote his report of the accident to his superior. Top management decided to go to court to fight the lawsuit against them for damages. But to the report writer's chagrin, the

Legal Department reversed their decision after reading his report.

Why? He had stated that the accident took place on October 16 rather than October 15 (simply a typo, he assured me). Because of that one inaccuracy, his supervisors pointed out, the plaintiff would question every other detail in the investigation. His company settled out of court.

Second, check the spelling of company names and individuals' names, and use correct titles. People get offended when you don't consider them important enough to phone a receptionist for the correct spelling and title.

Another consideration in checking for accuracy: Have you overstated the case anywhere? Understatement impresses much more than overstatement. Overstatement begs the reader to be skeptical. Consider this comment from a stranger, "I heard the funniest story yesterday—you won't believe it. You really won't." Your first thought usually is, "Oh, yeah?" And after he or she tells the story, there's always the letdown—the that-wasn't-so-funny feeling. Give the reader the facts; let him tell you how impressed he is.

Now for completeness. Would a case study or illustration (such as the two I just used) help? Novelists and playwrights make abstractions like greed and loyalty understandable by showing how these attitudes destroy or strengthen a particular family. Rather than quoting farm price indexes, the President tells of a specific Iowa farmer's crop failures. Rather than merely giving cure rates for leukemia, the journalist interviews a victim about his hope for recovery.

Recently, a speaker to a businessmen's group put things in perspective for "those in Washington who don't really know what a billion dollars is."

- one billion seconds ago, the first atomic bomb had not been exploded.
- one billion minutes ago, Christ was still on earth.
- one billion hours ago, men were still living in caves.
- yet one billion dollars ago in terms of government spending was yesterday.

Business writing as well as business speaking benefits by such illustrations; the bare facts do not always illuminate the whole story.

As for authority, any time you can find an "expert" to underscore your conclusions, or can survey to substantiate majority opinion, or can research printed sources to find documentation, you will have added weight to your arguments.

Use an exact quote when (1) the idea is not generally accepted, (2) the idea is original with a particular person, or (3) the thought is particularly well phrased. And quotes should be short and to the point; a four-line quote gets more attention than a twenty-line quote. Paraphrase the context and qualifications; use ellipses when necessary; then quote the pithy statement.

ELIMINATE REPETITIOUS DETAILS, BUT RETAIN FIRST-CHOICE WORDS

Cut out details or paragraphs that say what you have already made obvious. Repetition can be a problem, particularly when you make "Procedures" a separate section from "Results." Repetition also becomes a problem with a lengthy summary or introduction. Better to begin with the summary, the conclusions, and the recommendations, and omit an introduction altogether. Most introductory material is already known and can usually be woven into appropriate parts of the "body" anyway.

Don't worry, however, about repetitious words. In school, you have been given this advice: Instead of saying "evaluation" over and over, write "survey" or "opinion" or "conclusion." The teacher's motive was to get you to add variety and to build your vocabulary.

The holdover to that advice in business writing is something like the following: "In order for all parties to have incentive to cancel these arrangements and enter new ones, subsequent contracts should qualify for the maximum lawful price." Does "arrangements" mean "contracts" or other working arrangements?

"Table I summarizes the production values at each site; the evaluation does not include the Malcolmson project." Is Table I the same thing as the evaluation, or are they two different items?

Avoid repetitious details, but stick to your first-choice words; repetition is always preferable to miscommunication.

PARAGRAPH BY IDEA AND FOR EYE APPEAL

Consider coherence. Does the paragraph flow? Are irrelevant details buried in the middle of an otherwise organized paragraph?

Consider length. Generally, the paragraph should complete the subject at hand. One idea, one paragraph. However, the paragraph must also have eye appeal; long paragraphs tire the reader and make the material look too complex. On the other hand, short, choppy paragraphs cause the reader to lose the thread of an argument.

In general, continue a paragraph until you finish a thought; if, however, length becomes a problem, break the paragraph at a logical point. If you're giving five reasons why the computer is adequate, put three reasons in one paragraph, two in the following. Or if each reason will require a three-to-four-sentence explanation, devote one paragraph to each reason.

There is no minimum or maximum paragraph length. Do unto your reader as you would have him do unto you.

USE INFORMATIVE HEADINGS AND ADEQUATE WHITE SPACE

Good headings, like frequent paragraphs, are a courtesy to the reader because they make it easy to relocate details or to skim. Headings such as "Introduction," "Discussion," or "Justification" tell the reader very little unless you make further breaks with more specifics. Make headings informative, a capsule phrase of the major point to follow. Examples: "Torque-Turn Test Results," "Schedule for Microfilming Permanent Records," "Decreased Sales in Chicago."

Figure 14 will serve as a guide for heading placement that will allow you to break down materials as many as five times. Rarely will you need more divisions. Note that ' is arrangement lets

AUDIT FOR PERIOD ENDED JUNE 30, 1982
General Findings

Explanation follows here. . . .
General Ledger
Explanation follows here. . . .
Marketing
Strategy. Explanation follows here. . . .
Top Customers. Explanation follows here. . . .
Guaranty Files
Unissued Titled Policies. Explanation follows here. . . .
Missing Support Documents. Explanation follows here and
continues until necessary to break down again. In this case,
the writer should underline his key point and run the word or
phrase into the complete sentence, as the following show.
File No. SQ11-828 contains no evidence of the claim referred
to in the lien.
File No. DB-12-333 is missing an authorized statement of. . . .

Figure 14. Heading placement.

your reader understand major and minor points on any one page merely by skimming the headings.

Finally, don't forget to leave adequate white space between divisions. A crowded page makes written material look too complex to read. But adequate white space tempts the reader to wade into the water because it promises time to come up for a breath before the next lap.

In summary, to edit for content, follow these guides: Throughout the report or letter, stick with the angle of major interest to your reader. Make sure the proportion of written materials devoted to each idea indicates the importance of that idea. Recheck all figures for accuracy. Illuminate your ideas with illustrations or examples when necessary. Add authority to your proposals or arguments with support from the experts, from the majority, or from test results. Avoid repetitious details from section to section of the report, but retain your first-choice words.

Paragraph by idea and for eye appeal. As a courtesy and temptation to your reader, use informative, correctly placed headings as well as plenty of white space.

EDIT FOR GRAMMAR

Grammar rules are not static; they reflect usage, changing as life-styles change. A few strict grammarians still insist that "advise" cannot mean "inform," as in "advise me of any change of plans." "Advise" traditionally means to give counsel or advice. But the above business usage has been so common that dictionaries now give "inform" as a meaning for "advise."

This acknowledgment of change is not to discount grammar rules. Grammatical correctness is a matter of both clarity and image. Business writers frequently smile at grammatical blunders in the work of colleagues and competitors and on this basis classify the authors, sometimes unjustly, as to their expertise in other areas. But even more important than an unfavorable personal or company image, grammatical errors render an unclear message.

To freshen your memory on grammatical structure, review the basic sentence elements below:

MAJOR ELEMENTS OF THE SENTENCE

The major elements of the sentence are the subject, the verb, the object (direct or indirect), and the complement (subjective or objective).

The *complete subject* names whom or what you are referring to. This who or what is usually a noun or a pronoun plus the additional words that describe or limit its meaning. The *simple subject* is the person, place, thing, or idea without the descriptive or limiting words. For example:

The *employee* hired last	will make the trip.
Los Angeles	offers the most attractive clientele for our purposes.

| The company-owned computer *equipment* | has been depreciated at an annual 10 percent. |
| Cost-center budgeting | is the process of identifying individual managers with their performance. |

The *complete predicate* tells something about the subject. The major word in the predicate is the *verb*. This verb tells what the subject does, has, or is. For example:

Our lab technicians	*participated* in the Billings investigation with renewed determination.
The first construction project similar to this one	*consisted* of three 80-foot-by-750-foot piers.
The task force's major recommendation	*is* the information processing and the interconnection of technologies through telecommunications.

A sentence may be complete with only a subject and a verb: Activities slowed. He disapproves. Temperatures stabilize.

The problem with verbs is that they are often confused with verbals (infinitives, gerunds, and participles).

An *infinitive* is the word "to" plus a verb, and it serves as a noun, adjective, or adverb in the sentence. For example:

To complete these tables is a waste of time. (noun)
The tables *to show* income have been altered. (adjective)
He altered the facts *to prove* the experiment a success. (adverb)

A *gerund* is a verb plus -ing, and it serves as a noun in the sentence. For example:

Drilling is going slowly. (noun, subject)
Brown hates *compiling* these quarterly reports. (noun, direct object)

A *participle* is a verb plus -ing or -ed, and it serves as an adjective in the sentence. For example:

These graphs *illustrating* our project are being questioned by the programmers. (adjective, modifying "graphs")

This *completed* audit has been challenged by all parties who have an interest in the override. (adjective, modifying "audit")
Finishing the work two weeks early, James Duncan rescheduled that assignment for mid-June. (adjective, modifying "James Duncan")

Never confuse a verb with one of the above verbals, or you may write a fragment rather than a complete sentence.

The *direct object* receives the action of the verb or shows the result of the action. For example:

They reduced construction *time* by pile-driving.
He placed the *cage* outside the longitudinal holes.
Technicians assembled the *equipment* in functional order despite the previously discussed layout.

Notice that the direct object always answers "what" about the verb. They reduced *what*? He placed *what*? Technicians assembled *what*?

The *indirect object* names the receiver of the direct object. The indirect object is used with verbs of asking, giving, or telling. (In the examples below, the *indirect objects* precede the *direct objects):*

My assistant brought *me* the accumulated *balances* as of March 31.
We sent their *representative* an *ultimatum* and are waiting for their response.
Send *me* the shipping *instructions* to return the material as soon as possible.

The *subject complement* follows a linking (intransitive) verb and tells something about the subject of the sentence. Linking verbs are verbs incomplete in themselves—is, are, were, been, appear, become, seem, look, etc. You could never say, "My client seems" and have a complete thought as you would with a complete (transitive) verb such as "My client approves." For example:

Their manager becomes *disgruntled* at every mention of the promotional rally scheduled for next summer.

These policies seem more *outrageous* with each revision.

The basic component of that budget is the detailed expense *classification*.

The *objective complement* tells about the direct object of the sentence. For example:

He considered the project a *waste* of time due to a lack of financial commitment to the follow-up activities.

The preliminary draft kept the boss *preoccupied*.

Mr. Weymeyer proved the precautionary measures *unnecessary* in that the temperatures decreased without artificial stimulus.

These four elements—subject, verb, objects, complements—form the skeleton of all English sentences. You may or may not have objects or complements, but you must have a subject and a verb.

SECONDARY ELEMENTS OF THE SENTENCE

Adjectives and adverbs, two secondary elements of the sentence, are the flesh around the bones.

An *adjective* modifies (describes) a noun or a pronoun. For example:

Spiral reinforcement will be *the same quality* steel.

All data-processing employees should report to *this first* meeting.

This lengthy procedure has been detailed once again for *obvious safety* reasons.

An *adverb* modifies (describes) a verb, adjective, another adverb, or the sentence as a whole. An adverb tells when, where, why, or how something was done. For example:

Frank Broughton rechecked each graph *extensively before* forwarding it to the Editorial Department.

Our engineers *blatantly* refused to take on the project, insisting that the reassigned funds would be a problem.

The *much*-publicized policy has eliminated tardiness in his area of responsibility.

Candidly, I cannot fulfill the obligations within his time limit.

An *independent clause* contains a subject and a predicate and makes a complete thought. For example:

We have paid drilling advances to all producers in the South Padre Island area.

A *dependent clause* contains a subject and a predicate but does not make a complete statement by itself. It depends on the main (independent) clause to complete its meaning. For example:

Although the samples were contaminated, he recorded all the results.

Sentences with one clause are *simple.* Sentences with more than one clause can be categorized as *complex, compound,* or *compound-complex.* Simple sentences contain only one clause. For example:

Simple (one clause)
Donald Barton rechecked and relabeled all the bar graphs from each survey.
Complex (one independent clause, one dependent clause)
Because McWayte had mentioned the mistakes earlier, he rechecked and relabeled all the bar graphs from each survey.
Compound (two independent clauses)
Mr. Hyde thinks the decision is inconsistent with company policy, and he wants to calculate retroactively the interest on all such payments.
Compound-complex (two independent clauses, at least one dependent clause)
Fred Turpin included the applicable interest, and then he modified the conflicting policy, which seemed outdated.

A clause can take the place of either a major or a secondary sentence element. For example:

Whoever wants the project of coordinating the collection efforts may volunteer. (The italicized dependent clause serves as the subject of the independent clause.)

Please tell his secretary *that he will not be in today.* (The italicized dependent clause serves as the direct object of the independent clause.)

Tell anyone *who enters the warehouse* about the contamination. (The italicized dependent clause serves as an adjective limiting the meaning of "anyone" in the independent clause.)

(For additional help with grammar, study the Grammar Glossary, Appendix C.)

As a test of your faith in the grammatical structure reviewed above, commit yourself to keeping the Ten Commandments of Grammar below:

COMMANDMENT 1: THOU SHALT NOT DANGLE VERBALS

A participial verbal phrase serves as an adjective and must modify a noun or a pronoun. An introductory participial phrase usually attaches to the first noun that follows in the main clause. For example:

> *Incorrect:* As instructed in our phone conversation on March 21, his order was increased to four hundred pocket binders.

This sentence says that "his order" was instructed on the phone.

Passive voice is the culprit most of the time; it brings a passel of problems (as you'll see before you finish the editing step). Passive voice means that the subject of the sentence *receives* the action of the verb. With an active-voice sentence, the subject *does* the action of the verb:

> *Active*   Management rejected our plan.
> *Passive:*   Our plan was rejected by management.
> *Active:*   All parties signed the contracts.
> *Passive:*   The contracts were signed by all parties.

Dangling-verbal errors can be corrected on most occasions by sticking to an active-voice construction:

> *Correct:*   As instructed in our phone conversation March 21, we have adjusted his order accordingly.
> *Incorrect:* Having secured all windows and doors, the storage facility was vacated for the night. (The storage facility secured its own windows and doors?)
> *Correct:*   Having secured all windows and doors, the men vacated the storage facility for the night.

Danglers can also be corrected by rewording the sentence to eliminate the verbal:

Correct: The storage facility, with all windows and doors secured, was vacated for the night.

Incorrect: Assuming the previous values then, the revised cooling rate is given in Table 8. (The revised cooling rate assumed the previous values?)

Correct: Assuming the previous values then, we have revised the cooling rate as given in Table 8.

Correct: The revised cooling rate based on these assumed previous values is given in Table 8.

Don't be confused when the same error occurs at the end of the sentence:

Incorrect: Security is inefficient when deliveries are made *leaving doors open for long periods of time.*
(Deliveries leave doors open?)

Correct: Security is inefficient when deliverymen leave doors open for long periods of time.

Although most readers will understand your meaning when you have a dangling verbal, the error makes you look silly, as in this example: "Dangling free over the hole, the workmen attached the wire rope to the drum." (The workmen dangled free? Probably not.)

COMMANDMENT 2: THOU SHALT NOT WRITE FRAGMENTS FOR COMPLETE SENTENCES

Fragments are word groups rather than complete sentences. Usually, these word groups are fragments because they contain no verb for the subject in the main clause. For example:

The policies which have proven inadequate in the past and have even infuriated some employees. ("Have proven" and "have infuriated" are verbs of the minor "which" clause. "Policies" has no verb.)

Although there is no clear authority for any of these procedures outlined in the manual. (The subordinate conjunction "although" introduces a dependent clause. This dependent clause cannot stand alone as a complete sentence. If you mean "although" as "on the other hand," you must separate it from the rest of the clause with a comma.)

To correct these fragments, either add a verb or connect a dependent clause or phrase to an independent clause. For example:

Fragment: The lease should be maintained. Although there is no clear Texas authority.

Revised: The lease should be maintained, although there is no clear Texas authority.

Fragment: We do not think it would be economical to consider a used spectrometer. Because the cost is not much less than for a new one.

Revised: We do not think it would be economical to consider a used spectometer, because the cost is not much less than for a new one.

COMMANDMENT 3: THOU SHALT USE PARALLEL STRUCTURE

Parallelism refers to like structure of words, phrases, or clauses within a sentence. Unparallel parts of a sentence can lead to confusion. For example:

Unparallel: One of the benefits of the call-forwarding system is that the initiator has complete control of when it can be done, to whom it can be forwarded, and for any length of time.

Parallel: One of the benefits of the call-forwarding system is that the initiator has complete control *of when, to whom,* and *for what time* the forwarding can be done.

(The three equal ideas are equal in construction—three prepositional phrases.)

Unparallel: When I phoned McConnel, he asked me to review those calculations, to select fifteen VPL contracts for his review, the purchase agreements with OSD, and to verify the volumes and prices.

(What about the purchase agreements with OSD? Are they to be reviewed by the writer or selected for McConnel's review?)

Parallel: When I phoned McConnel, he asked me to review those calculations, to select fifteen VPL contracts for his review, *to review* the purchase agreements with OSD, and to verify the volumes and prices.

Any parallel form (all adjective phrases, all clauses, all infinitives, etc.) will work as long as the equal ideas are given equal billing in the sentence:

Unparallel: Technologists with good experience and knowledgeable . . .
Parallel: Technologists with good experience and knowledge . . .
Parallel: Technologists who have experience and knowledge . . .
Parallel: Experienced and knowledgeable technologists . . .

Even lists sound better when parallel. Note the difference in the two below:

Unparallel
Fuel-air ratio out-of-balance (*noun phrase, then adjective*)
Insufficient pin and bushing lubrication (*adjective phrase, then noun phrase*)
Lubrication of cylinder insufficient (*noun phrase, then adjective*)
BTU's too high (*noun, then adjective*)
Maintenance procedures not followed (*noun phrase, then verbal*)
Ignition malfunction (*noun phrase*)
Peak balance was improper (*complete sentence*)

Parallel (the adjective or adjective phrase comes first, then the noun or noun phrase)
Out-of-balance fuel-air ratio
Insufficient pin and bushing lubrication
Insufficient cylinder lubrication
High BTU's
Improper maintenance procedures
Malfunctioning ignition
Improper peak balance

Unparallel sentences and lists grate on the ear as well as obscure meaning.

COMMANDMENT 4: THOU SHALT MAKE PRONOUNS AGREE IN NUMBER WITH THEIR ANTECEDENTS

This error, usually a careless one by a writer who knows better, also leads to clarity problems. For example:

Unclear: These tools arrived with the later order. Therefore, we were unable to use it to perform those tests. (He couldn't use the tools or the entire order? If you were working in the Shipping Department, what would you return to the sender for a refund?)

Revised: These *tools* arrived with the later order. Therefore, we were unable to use *them* to perform those tests.

Unclear: Each supervisor should inform his employees of the new procedures. They should also develop a checklist for monitoring the equipment. (Who should develop the checklist? "They" in the second sentence may refer to "employees," but the word "also" in the second sentence suggests that the writer is still talking to each supervisor.)

Revised: Each *supervisor* should inform his employees of the new procedures. *He* should also develop a checklist for monitoring the equipment.

COMMANDMENT 5: THOU SHALT MAKE VERBS AGREE WITH THEIR SUBJECTS

A singular subject calls for a singular verb; a plural subject calls for a plural verb. Remember that to make a *noun* plural, you add an "s." But to make a verb plural, you remove the "s." For example:

The experiment proves our theory.
The experiments prove our theory.

In short, simple sentences you can usually depend on your ear for subject-verb agreement. However, long sentences with complicated structure may cause problems. Study the following ten sentences and select the appropriate word. Then refer to the correct answers and explanations that follow the sentences.

Sentences

1. The group of employees who recently became eligible for these benefits (have, has) steadily grown in the past two months.
2. Also helpful in this analysis and related to the study of adjacent support (is, are) cases involving underground water rights.
3. The management (meet, meets) at two-thirty to exchange data.

4. Neither Wayne Brown nor his two associates (have, has) given us the go-ahead for the project.
5. None of the tools used for the job (was, were) accurately serviced before the workers began.
6. Data (show, shows) that the project is doomed from the beginning.
7. One third of the samples (has, have) been sprayed.
8. A person who is liable under the rule stated in Subsection G is also liable for harm to artificial additions that (result, results) from each subsidence.
9. This is one of the accounts that (is, are) frequently paid late.
10. Bad weather, together with faulty tools, (complicates, complicate) the analysis and sample-taking.

Answers and Explanations

1. *has* "Group" is the subject. Don't be confused by words, phrases, or clauses coming between the subject and the verb of the main clause.
2. *are* Watch out for inverted sentence order. Writers of English sentences most often use the subject-verb-object construction, but don't be confused with a less frequent construction.
3. *meets* In business usage, collective nouns take singular verbs.
4. *have* When you have the conjunctions either-or/neither-nor, treat them as separate units. If the subject of both units is singular, use a singular verb: "Neither Brown nor Smith *has* transferred out of the office." If, however, one of the units happens to be plural (as in sentence 4), place the plural unit last and make the verb plural.
5. *were* "None" is an indefinite pronoun; that means it can be either singular or plural. Some writers incorrectly insist that *none* is a contraction for *not one*; *none* can, however, have either of two meanings: *not one* or *not any*. Make your choice according to the pronoun's referent. In this case, none refers to "tools." But you would write, "None of the nitrogen *is* missing." "All" and "some" follow the same rule. You would write, "Some of the

money *is* missing," but "Some of the coins *are* missing."

6. Either is correct, depending on meaning. Actually, "datum" is the Latin singular, but common usage says "data" can be either singular or plural. "Data show" means that you are referring to more than one piece of information. "Data shows" means that you are referring either to one piece of information or to the body of information as a single unit.

7. *have* With fractions, check the context for meaning. When referring to the samples individually (as in this case), use plural. But when referring to the samples as a unit, use singular: "One third of the samples goes to Baltimore, and one third stays here."

8. *results* You must decide on the referent for "that"— "harm" or "additions." In this case, "that" probably refers to harm, because the sentence talks of liability for damage. But a reader could build a strong argument for "additions" as the antecedent for "that." Again, grammar and clarity go hand in hand. Only the verb choice tells the reader your meaning.

9. Either is correct, depending on meaning. If you mean that *this* account is the only late one, the referent of "that" is "one," and the proper verb choice is "is." If you mean, however, that his account is only one of several late accounts, the referent of "that" is "accounts," and the proper verb choice is "are." Confusing? Just think how you could mislead a reader with the incorrect choice.

10. *complicates* "Together with faulty tools" is a parenthetical element—like an appositive. Don't be mislead by asides and additional explanatory material. Locate the real subject, "bad weather" in this case.

To obey this commandment about subject-verb agreement, keep one overriding caution in mind: Most people write by ear— that is, they do not consciously ponder verb choice. The danger of error is most prevalent in sentences containing "that" or "which" clauses, because your ear will make the verb after "that" or "which" agree with the last noun before it. And the noun immediately preceding may or may not be its antecedent. In

68

addition to dangerous "that" or "which" clauses, note the differences in meanings determined by verb choice in sentences such as 5 and 6.

Your verb choice may be the reader's only clue to your meaning.

COMMANDMENT 6: THOU SHALT NOT CHANGE TENSES AND MOODS UNNECESSARILY

Switching tenses and moods, like an error in subject-verb agreement, is rather common. But unnecessary switches mislead. For example:

> The term "use" *is defined* broadly and *would include* sales, processing, and manufacturing.

Let's say the writer of the above sentence is explaining to his supervisor the contents of Document A. Is the term "use" only broadly defined in the document, and is the writer adding his own opinion that "use" includes sales, processing, and manufacturing? Or does Document A specifically mention that "use" refers to sales, processing, and manufacturing? When the writer slips into the conditional mood (would), his comments sound like opinion rather than fact.

> *Clearer:* The term "use" *is defined* broadly and *includes* sales, processing, and manufacturing.

Present:	We analyze the samples each day.
Past:	We analyzed the samples yesterday.
Future:	We will analyze the samples tomorrow.
Present perfect:	We have analyzed the samples each day this week.
Past perfect:	We had analyzed the samples before he called.
Future perfect:	We will have analyzed the samples before he calls tomorrow.

Indicative-mood verbs make declarative statements of fact:
We analyze each sample.

Subjunctive-mood verbs state ideas or events that are contrary to fact or conditional: We would analyze the samples if we had the right chemicals.

Imperative-mood verbs give commands:
Analyze the samples.

> The gas *was* analyzed by injecting 2 cc's of water and withdrawing 2 cc's of gas with a calibrated syringe. A carrier gas *transports* the sample through the column, which *separates* the gas components before they *reach* the detector.

Has the gas mentioned in the first sentence been analyzed at a time prior to the present procedure in the second sentence? The tense mix suggests that. Or perhaps the second sentence represents a pause in the procedure and is merely an explanation of what is happening at this point in the process.

> *Clearer:*   The gas *is* analyzed . . .

Of course, some tense changes are necessary:

> Our company *initiated* the process in the 1950s; each employee *has* since *reaped* the benefits.

Don't be lax about tense and mood changes.

COMMANDMENT 7: THOU SHALT PUNCTUATE CORRECTLY

Columnist Elizabeth Zwart in the *Des Moines Tribune* writes: "The older I grow, the less important the comma becomes. Let the reader catch his own breath."

A humorous statement, but the business writer knows that the comma serves a higher purpose than letting the reader catch his breath. In addition to courtesy, punctuation's purpose is clarity. Assuming periods give few people problems, I'll move to the more complicated marks.

Commonly Used and Abused Comma Rules

To introduce:

• Use a comma after an introductory word.

Actually, both hardware systems would serve equally well.

• Use a comma after an introductory phrase.

Having completed the tests, we removed our equipment.
On the contrary, I specifically invited him to the meeting.

• Use a comma after an introductory adverbial clause.

When I requested these records, I found that they had been sent to the Dallas office.

To separate:

• Use a comma between two independent clauses joined by a coordinate conjunction (and, but, nor, or, for, so, yet).

We compiled the data two weeks before the due date, and then we forwarded the rough draft to this office for final interpretation and approval.

I prefer a pre-award meeting with the vendor, but Tim Hyatt wants to begin construction immediately.

• Use a comma to separate items in a series.

The retrieval service will give summaries of the articles, current or historical market quotes, company profiles, and 10-K extracts.

To enclose:

• Use a comma to cut away nonessential (nonrestrictive) clauses and phrases from the rest of the sentence.

The Records Committee recommends that we implement a Vital Records Protection Program for all organizational units, especially those in the New York offices, and develop a procedures manual after the "pilot" effort. ("Especially those in the New York offices" is nonessential, additional information.)

This bid does not cover the Houston jobs, which were contracted for after June 15. (The bid does not cover any Houston jobs. The last clause set off by a comma is nonessential explanation.)
This bid does not cover the Houston jobs which were contracted for after June 15. (Without a comma cutting away the last clause, the reader knows that this is essential information that restricts the meaning of "jobs." This bid does not cover Houston jobs contracted for after June 15, but it does cover jobs contracted for *before* June 15.)

This payment involves secretarial jobs where this policy has been in effect since 1975. (Payment involves only jobs where the policy has been in effect since 1975. Jobs where this policy was put into effect earlier are not included.)
This payment involves secretarial jobs, where this policy has been

in effect since 1975. ("This payment" involves only secretarial jobs. The comma to cut off the last clause tells the reader only additional, nonessential information.)

To introduce, separate, enclose—the comma does more than help a reader catch his breath. Some grammarians insist that "which" in the above examples should be "that" when the words are essential or restrictive to the noun. Frequently, however, the lowly comma carries the total weight of clarity on its shoulder.

Queer Quotes

Rules about quote marks often bring resistance because some writers who have been out of school awhile and have forgotten the rules depend on logic. And logic fails here:

- Commas and periods *always* go *inside* quote marks— regardless of meaning.

If these figures came from "Subsection 2," please retabulate them.
In this case, there was no "wanton conduct."

- Semicolons and colons *always* go *outside* quote marks—regardless of meaning.

These authorizations should be filed beginning with the letter "k"; they must also be numbered consecutively.
He issued an "ultimatum": Sign or resign.

- Question marks go *inside or outside*—depending on meaning.

Who can tell me why this particular account is considered a "bomb"?

Clayton ends every statement with "But why are we sidetracking here?"

In the preceding examples with commas and periods, reason tells you that the comma should go *after* the quote ("If the figures came from Subsection 2",) because the comma sets off the entire introductory clause. But logic doesn't hold here; a rule is a rule is a rule.

Having made my point, I'll recant to say that there are exceptions: *some* legal documents and anything from the U.S. Government Printing Office. In these two instances, quote-mark usage always depends on meaning.

Strong Semicolons

- Semicolons take the place of missing conjunctions.

This will be an ongoing process; it will not end when the consultant's contract is completed.

- Semicolons precede connective adverbs used as conjunctions (for example: however, consequently, moreover, therefore, hence, thus).

A micrographics system is not an income-producing program; however, the costs are significantly lower than those of conventional records handling. Notice the comma after "however." (Note: The use of *"however"* does not require a semicolon in the following sentence because the word does not separate two independent clauses. *However* in this case is merely an interrupting word rather than a connective adverb: "The costs, however, are not significantly lower.")

- Semicolons replace commas to separate items in a series when the items already have internal commas.

Confusing: Your manager stopped by to deliver the following supplies: Forms 302, which have been on back order for six months, two boxes of stencils, the notebooks, minus the damaged pages, forms 1601.

Clearer: Your manager stopped by to deliver the following supplies: Forms 302, which have been on back order for six months; two boxes of stencils; the notebooks, minus the damaged pages; Forms 1601.

Uncommon Colons

- Use a colon as you would a semicolon—when the second clause amplifies the first.

Management's ideas are always the same: Take the risk.

• Use a colon when a series follows.

Turn in the following tables to the typist: Table 8, Table 10, Table 14, Table 17.

Daring Dashes

• Use dashes to set off parenthetical material—information nonessential to the rest of the sentence.

He cannot—and this is strictly a personal opinion—handle the job as well as Tom Bohommen did last year.

• If the context calls for a dash where a comma would ordinarily be, omit the comma.

Because the figures had not been charted—the reason for this will be presented later—the report has been delayed.

• If the parenthetical element requires a question mark or exclamation point, use it.

Smith's plan—can he have promotion on his mind?—calls for increased responsibility for that position.

COMMANDMENT 8: THOU SHALT CHOOSE APPROPRIATE WORDS AND PHRASES

Study the meanings of the frequently misused words and phrases given in Figure 15. Edit such errors from your work.

OFTEN MISUSED WORDS AND PHRASES

accept   to receive
except   not including
affect   to influence
effect   to cause, a result
aggravate   to add to
irritate   to vex, to annoy
all ready   everyone, everything is ready
already   previously
all right   agreed, OK, all are correct
alright   unacceptable usage

all together everyone, everything is together
altogether completely, without exception
allusion a reference
illusion false impression
among more than two involved
between two involved
amount mass or volume
number things counted
biannual twice a year
biennial every two years, or continuing for two years
semiannual twice a year
complement to make complete
compliment to congratulate
comprise to embrace, not "comprise of"
continual regular, but interrupted
continuous constant and uninterrupted succession
criteria plural
criterion singular
data singular or plural
datum singular
different from correct
different than incorrect
disinterested impartial
uninterested not interested in
fact verified past events or statistics
      never "the fact that energy *may* be . . ."
      never "*evidence* points to the fact that . . ."
      never "he's got his facts *wrong*"
farther distance, can be measured
further time or quantity that cannot easily be measured
finalize pompous, ambiguous verb (negotiated? signed? terminated?)
formally in a formal manner
formerly previously
infer listener or reader infers
implies speaker or writer implies
its possessive pronoun
it's it is
less quantity not easily measured, e.g., "less time"
fewer number
mean average
median halfway
mode value around which the items tend to concentrate

> **operative**   working
> **operational**   refers to causal factor, ready to work
> **personal**   belonging to a particular person
> **personnel**   people
> **phenomenon**   singular
> **phenomena**   plural
> **practical**   useful or workable, as opposed to theoretical
> **practicable**   possible or feasible
> **principle**   a general rule or truth
> **principal**   chief
> **stationary**   fixed position
> **stationery**   writing material
> **unique**   without like or equal (There can be no degrees of
>   uniqueness—not "more unique," not "most unique.")
> **utilize**   pompous, prefer use
> **wise**   in the manner of (not to be used as a pseudosuffix such as
> "taxwise," "pricewise," "businesswise")

Figure 15. Become aware of misused words in your own writing.

COMMANDMENT 9: THOU SHALT SPELL CORRECTLY

When you don't know that you don't know how a word is spelled, you don't know to check the dictionary! But awareness solves that problem. Below is a list of frequently misspelled words; to make yourself aware of words you habitually misspell, underline the correct spellings and then check the answers in Appendix D.

accessible, acessible

accomodate, accommodate

accurate, acurrate

achieve, acheive

allotted, alloted

analyze, analize

antequated, antiquated

apparatus, aparratus

arguement, argument

mecanics, mechanics

mileage, milage

ninety, ninty

ocassionally, occasionally

occurred, occured

occurrence, occurence

parallel, paralell

perform, preform

permanent, permenant

bulletin, bulliten
buoyant, bouyant
category, catagory
changeable, changable
commitment, committment
concensus, consensus
controlled, controled
definite, definate
dependent, dependant
description, discretion
descrepancy, discrepancy
dispel, dispell
embarrass, embarass
exceed, excede
existence, existance
exorbitant, exhorbitant
fourty, forty
insistent, insistant
inadvertent, inadvertant
indispensible, indispensable
judgment, judgement
license, licence
maintenance, maintanence

perserverance, perseverance
personnel, personel
precede, preceed
privilege, privelege
procede, proceed
proceedure, procedure
quandary, quandery
porportion, proportion
recede, receed
receive, recieve
repetition, repitition
separate, seperate
seize, sieze
sieve, seive
similar, similiar
succeed, succede
superintendent, superintendant
supercede, supersede
technique, techneque
transferred, transfered
vacuum, vaccuum
whether, wheather

Every time you use these words, or any other words whose spelling you're unsure of, check a dictionary or put a question mark over them and ask your typist to check for you.

In addition to these difficult words, misspelling frequently involves apostrophes and hyphens.

Be Positive About Apostrophes

- Use apostrophes to show possession with nouns. Make the noun either singular or plural first, and then add the apostrophe.

The consultant's contract (one consultant)
The consultants' contract (two consultants)
This is Fran Potts' new office. (In this case and in the sentence above, the "s" after the apostrophe is dropped for sound reasons, because the noun already ends in "s.")

Brown and Smith's work (one project, joint ownership)
Brown's and Smith's work (two projects)

- Do not use apostrophes with possessive pronouns. These pronouns are already possessive—his, hers, yours, theirs.

The company agrees to hold *its* employees blameless. (Do not confuse with "it's," which means it is.)

- Use apostrophes (possessive form) before gerunds.

Be aware of the *court's* construing the damage as a temporary injury. (Remember that the gerund phrase "construing the damage as a temporary injury" takes the place of a noun. Substitute the word "decision" for the gerund phrase to see why possessive form is necessary here.)

Hairy Hyphens

- Use a hyphen between two related adjectives when they precede a noun.

Use a chilled-water valve. (This refers to a certain type of valve made especially for chilled water. Without the hyphen the sentence would refer to a water valve that had been chilled by running cold water through it for a specified time. Again, correct grammar means clarity.)

- Do not use a hyphen between related adjectives when they follow a noun.

This is heavy-gauge pipe.
This pipe is heavy gauge.
Your men should follow the plan step by step.
Your men should follow the step-by-step plan.

Why all the hype about hyphens? Jay B. Rohrlick in his book *Work and Love* relates this governmental goof: A congressional clerk was instructed to write, "All foreign fruit-plants are free from duty." Instead he wrote, "All foreign fruit, plants are free from duty." The government lost two million dollars in import taxes before a new session of Congress could rectify the error.

No, this is not an infrequent mistake. A reporter for *The Wall Street Journal*, William E. Blundell, tells about another costly hyphen error. A supervisor at a government-run nuclear installation ordered radioactive rods cut into "10 foot long lengths." He got 10 rods, each a foot long—instead of the 10-foot lengths he needed. The actual dollar loss to the government was classified.

Where do you go for the final word on hyphenation? A recent, reputable dictionary is the best choice. Style manuals vary, but the majority agree that the prefix compounds pre-, post-, over-, under-, intra-, extra-, infra-, ultra-, sub-, super-, pro-, ant-, re-, un-, non-, semi-, pseudo-, supra-, co- should be joined to the root word without a hypen. The prefix compounds self-, half-, all-should be hyphenated. But let me repeat: Hyphenation varies from company to company, publisher to publisher, writer to writer. Some build a "pipe line"; others build a "pipe-line"; and still others build a "pipeline."

When two words frequently begin to be used together, they gradually appear hyphenated. When they are used almost exclusively together, the hyphen is dropped and they become one word. Who is to say at what month and year two words should become hyphenated or should drop their hyphen and become a single, unhyphenated word? My preference is the *Oxford Dictionary.*

COMMANDMENT 10: THOU SHALT NOT CLUTTER WITH CAPITALIZATION

I've stated this commandment negatively, because most writers use too many capital letters rather than too few.

Each Company agrees that, during each Accounting Period after the Completion Date, its Company's Throughput, which constitutes Initial Facility Throughput, shall not be less than the Company's Percentage.

The preceding sentence is no joke; it comes from a joint-venture agreement between two major oil companies.

All proper nouns (and their derivatives and abbreviations) such as product names, place names, individual names, and company names should be capitalized. The first word and all key words in titles—book titles, document titles, department titles, section titles, project titles, etc.—should be capitalized. First words in sentences should be capitalized. Anything else clutters. If you mean to emphasize a key word, underline rather than capitalize it.

Grammar and clarity are inseparable. Breaking any one of these Ten Commandments of Grammar may either muddy your message or mar your image.

To evaluate your understanding of these principles in editing for grammar, take the quiz in Appendix E.

EDIT FOR CLARITY

MEASURE READABILITY

The major hindrance to clear communication is complexity in the writing style rather than complexity of the idea. To eliminate this unnecessary barrier, researchers have developed several methods of measuring the reading level of written material. Robert Gunning's formula (see Figure 16) is one of the easiest to use.

When you apply his formula to a sample of writing, the resulting Fog Index represents the grade level at which you're writing. A Fog Index of 10 to 12 is ideal. You may be surprised to know that no popular magazine in the United States is written above the twelfth-grade reading level. *The Atlantic Monthly* and *The New Yorker*, "literary" magazines, have a Fog Index of 12. *Time, Newsweek*, and *The Wall Street Journal* average 11.

Of course, these magazines are all aimed primarily at college graduates. The issue is energy. Why force the reader to spend time and effort in deciphering complex sentence structure when his energy can be channeled into understanding complex ideas?

Fog: The individual appointed to the jobsite field location with the responsibility for jobsite procurement, and to whom the purchasing function is thereby delegated, shall have the authority and the responsibility for acting in compliance with Corporate Procedure 6001 and adherence to the requirements of this

---

Step 1: *Count a hundred-word-sample of your writing* (Begin with the first word of a sentence and count exactly one hundred words. Count contractions and hyphenated words as one. Count numbers under four digits as one word, numbers over four digits as two words.)

Step 2: *Count the number of sentences in those hundred words and figure the average sentence length* (Independent clauses are counted as sentences, so you will have as many sentences as you have independent clauses. When the count stops in the middle of a sentence, estimate to the fraction, such as 0.3 or 0.5. 100 words ÷ 3.3 sentences = 30 words per sentence.)

Step 3: *Count the number of words with three or more syllables* (Exceptions: Do not count verb forms made three syllables by adding -ed or -es. Do not count proper nouns such as company or product names. Do not count compound words made of two simple words, such as "bookkeeper." Do not count the same word after it appears the first time, and do not count the -ses, -ed, ing, or -ly form of a word already counted once.)

Step 4: *Add the results of steps 2 and 3 and multiply by 0.4*

Example: 30 words per sentence
          $\underline{+\ 16}$ words of three or more syllables
              46
          $\underline{\times\ 0.4}$ fog factor
            18.4 Fog Index

The Fog Index is the number of years of education a person needs to read your material easily.

Figure 16. Robert Gunning's readability formula.

procedure. This person is authorized to make local purchase commitments without monetary limitations for materials, supplies, equipment, spare parts, and services required for job operational needs upon receipt of duly authorized requisitions within the approved job estimate. (82 words; For Index = 25.6)

Why make a reader read this paragraph twice to get the relatively simple message? To clear this passage of "fog," shorten the sentences and eliminate unnecessarily difficult words.

Revised: The jobsite buyer shall have the authority and responsibility outlined in Corporate Procedure 6001. With authorized requisitions, this person may buy locally all supplies, equipment, spare parts, and services within the limits of the approved job estimate. (38 words; Fog Index = 10.4)

Not only does foggy writing confuse and amuse, long sentences often camouflage important ideas:

There is a wide variation in their chemical content, which influences their heat content, and total sulfur can be determined only by heating to 800°C a coal sample combined with Eschka's Mixture.

Did you pick up on the idea that the variation in chemical content influences heat? Here's the same thought expressed in two sentences with both ideas getting equal billing:

The wide variation in their chemical content influences their heat content. Total sulfur can be determined only by heating to 800°C a coal sample combined with Eschka's Mixture.

To avoid buried ideas and unnecessary complexity, business sentences should average 15 to 20 words. Roughly, that means 2 to 2½ lines of either typewritten or handwritten material. To avoid exceeding a Fog Index of 12, you may have to compensate for a difficult vocabulary necessary for your field by using even shorter sentences than you ordinarily would write.

An average sentence of 17.5 words will not mean writing at an elementary level, such as in the following letter:

Dear Mr. Jones:
The Selection Board considers all local applicants for each new position. They carefully considered all candidates qualified for this New Orleans position. You were not one of those nominated for consideration. Management is limited in the number of candidates it may nominate. Competition is often very keen.

We are most appreciative of your interest in the position. You can be sure you will continue to be considered for other vacancies.

This letter averages less than 10 words per sentence. Revision into longer sentences still renders this letter at an easy reading level. The following letter averages 16 words per sentence.

82

NIEKRO PITCHES ASTROS TO 3-0 WIN OVER CARDS

The Houston Astros are brimming with confidence under the Astrodome.

More confidence than ever before? "Yes, due to maturity," say Joe Niekro, who pitched a 3-0 shutout over St. Louis Wednesday night for Houston's 11th straight home win and 12th success in 14 games overall. "The biggest challenge for us this year was getting off to a good start and, considering how many early games we had on the road, we did that. Now, we're just playing good, sound baseball every day."

(82 words)

The Houston Astros baseball team appears to be quite confident within the confines of the team's home facility, the Astrodome.

In response to the June 21 question by newspaper personnel with regard to the significant amount of confidence the team exuded in relationship to that formerly displayed by same, Joe Niekro, who delivered the sphere across the home plate achieving a 3-0 shutout over the St. Louis Cardinals Wednesday night for the Houston Astros' 11th consecutive victory and 12th successful feat in a total of 14 games overall, responded, "Affirmative, owing to the maturity achieved by all of us." Niekro went on to say, "The most extensive postulation for us during this particular baseball season proved to be a progressive and unimpaired initiation into our beginning confrontations. In view of the fact that we had a considerable number of games in various locations around the nation, we accomplished our initial goal. At the present time, a worthwhile, consistent game of baseball is being played by all of us on a continual basis."

(172 words)

Figure 17. A sports article from the *Houston Chronicle* and its counterpart translated into bureaucratese.

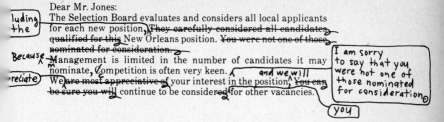

Although scientists are most vocal about their inability to write at readable levels, competent journalists for popular magazines frequently reword scientific journal articles for easier reading (see Figure 18).

When business readers consider a subject too technical, most likely the writing is at fault. Long sentences and difficult words make your reader work to decipher your words rather than to understand your ideas.

Clear writing demands clear thinking. Clarity, rather than gobbledygook, is a true mark of intelligence. Company policy manuals, instructional materials, and research reports written at appropriate reading levels, void of fog, could save businesses millions of dollars each year.

POSITION TO INDICATE EMPHASIS

The position of an idea suggests its importance. You can elevate an idea by placing it prominently, or bury it by placing it among a clutter of details (commonly know as "the fine print").

The *body position* of most prominence is the beginning. That's why a report should begin with conclusions and recommendations rather than a history of the project or procedures. Likewise, a letter should begin with the message, not a warm-up drill rehashing previous correspondence.

Buried Message:

Dear Mr. Brown:
This letter acknowledges receipt of your correspondence of July 9 in which you asked about the feasibility of coordinating our efforts on the Saudi project to be completed by our September

84

Figure 18. Journalists frequently find complex ideas in technical journals and rewrite them in clear prose for the lay reader.

target date. After reviewing your suggestions for coordinating our efforts, *I see no limitations in proceeding as you outlined.* . . .

Revised with the message in the position of emphasis:

Dear Mr. Brown:
After reviewing the suggestions in your July 9 letter, *I see no limitations in coordinating our efforts in the Saudi project.*

Paragraph position of most prominence is also at the beginning. A skimming reader would miss the main point in this paragraph:

Buried topic sentence:

Much of the gain in the use of oil and gas has been for transportation, household, and commercial uses for which coal is considerably less suitable. However, 27 percent of the oil and about 64 percent of the natural gas is used for industrial and electric utility purposes, many of which, from an efficiency standpoint, could be served equally well by coal. Oil and gas are preferred for convenience and cleanliness and, especially in the case of natural gas, for economic reasons. *But coal has other serious problems in competing for today's energy market*—the emission of particulate matter and sulfur dioxide. Technology is available for the control of particulates by electrostatic precipitators. However, despite numerous advertisements and claims to the contrary, up to today, April 20, 1973, no full-size, commercial-scale process for the removal of sulfur from stack gases has been operated successfully and continuously in the United States for a sufficiently long period of time to be considered fully proved. Some are reported to do the job when operating, but operations have been intermittent because of technical difficulties. Some foreign processes are reported to be successful, but questions remain as to whether their performance can meet United States conditions and requirements.

Fiction writers can shuffle topic sentence position for variety. But in business writing, the topic sentence, if at all possible, should come first in the paragraph, immediately after the transitional thought. When you read a paragraph that begins "Actually the two procedures are similar," you know exactly what you'll find in the body of the paragraph—a discussion of similarities.

With correctly placed topic sentences, busy readers can skim to find paragraphs that merit closer attention.

The *position in the sentence* of most prominence, many writers fail to realize, is at the end. The second strongest emphasis comes at the beginning. Clauses and phrases of least importance go in the middle. (Of course, this applies only in the placement of clauses, not words. Applied to single-clause sentences, that would mean that each word gets successively more important toward the end of the sentence.)

Forming a sentence without attention to this natural emphasis may mislead your reader about your intended message and the implications of that message.

Presently, John Monroe and Henry Jobe are writing controls and procedures so these out-of-balances can be monitored monthly and correcting entries can be made.

> In order to monitor those out-of-balances monthly and to enter necessary corrections, John Monroe and Henry Jobe are writing controls and procedures.

Either sentence sounds correct—and is, depending on your meaning. The first emphasizes why the controls and procedures are being written. The second emphasizes who is doing what about the problem.

> It may be necessary to shorten our retention period on the magazines that we currently house in order to reduce space requirements.

In this sentence, the emphasis is on why, "to reduce space requirements." But in the following sentence the emphasis is on what to do, "shorten our retention period."

> To reduce space requirements for magazines that we currently house, it may be necessary to shorten our retention period.

Note, also, that the least important clause is buried, as it should be, in the middle of the sentence.

Of course, when you intend the "which" or "that" clause to be an afterthought or aside, placing it at the end of the sentence is fine. In such sentences the reader knows what the emphasis is, no matter where the words are placed:

> The board will become discolored and movies will be affected, when we used the board as a screen.

The reader knows the main idea; the last clause just "hangs on," sounding weak and anticlimactic.

Possibly due to this oversight about emphasis, more so than with any other problem, we hear comments such as, "I know what you said, but I didn't know that you meant. . . ."

To communicate clearly, _you_ must decide where you want the emphasis to fall.

LINK TO SHOW PROPER RELATIONSHIPS

Analyze the logical flow of your words, phrases, or sentences, and join them properly to show their relationship to each other. Are both ideas of equal rank? Is one part of the sentence a result of the other? Is one clause a contradiction of the other? Is there a time relationship? Misjoined clauses and phrases confuse the reader.

What is the more important message in the following two sentences?

> The atomic absorption method which we use to determine trace elements in coal is a dry ashing-acid dissolution technique.
> The atomic absorption method, a dry ashing-acid dissolution technique, is what we use to determine trace elements.

In the first sentence the technique is more important because this information comes in the main clause. The linking word "which" introduces the minor clause containing the minor idea.

In the second sentence the main clause again tells the main idea—what they do with the technique, "determine trace elements." The fact that it is a "dry ashing-acid dissolution" is subordinated in a minor phrase in the middle of the sentence—the position of least emphasis. The "message" in the two sentences above is quite different.

In the following examples an improper linking "and" makes the message unclear:

> The tables are in chronological order of testing and contain the following information. (The "and" is like plus—this equals that. Are both ideas joined by "and" in this sentence equal?)

> The tables, in chronological order of testing, contain the following information. (Emphasis is on the information the tables contain because the "chronological order" is now only a phrase.)

> The tables, containing the following information, are in chronological order of testing. (Emphasis is on the chronological order because that idea is now in the main clause rather than in an equal phrase linked by "and.")

Nowhere is proper linking more important than in giving instructions.

> Turn the lever to the right *and* depress the cylinder which opens the air chamber. (Is this one action or two? The "and" is ambiguous.)
> Turn the lever to the right *while* depressing the cylinder which opens the air chamber. (Stating the proper time relationship makes the instruction clear.)

Turn the lever to the right, *thereby* depressing the cylinder which opens the air chamber. (One action. The depressed cylinder is a result of the first action.)

The linking word "or" can also obscure meaning.

Approximately two grams of whole coal or liquefaction residue, as received, was placed in the crucible.

Is whole coal the same as liquefaction residue? Or is the author talking about either of two elements? I had to ask the geologist who wrote this sentence, because not having an engineering background, I thought this distinction might be clear to someone in that field. No, the two items are not the same, he assured me, and no, the distinction wouldn't be clear unless an engineer specifically had experience with the liquefaction process.

To prevent misreading with the "or" link, add parentheses or use both correlative conjunctions:

This stress or the stress at the outer coupling will . . . (One stress or two?)

Either this stress *or* the stress at the outer coupling will . . . .

This stress (the stress at the outer coupling) will . . . .

If you want to show two ideas of equal rank, join them with a coordinate conjunction (and, but, or, nor, for, so, yet). If you want to connect a major idea to a minor idea, link with a subordinate conjunction (although, since, because, if, etc.) or a relative pronoun (which, that, what). If you want to show resulting action, use a linking word that conveys the cause-effect relationship (thereby, consequently, causing). If you need to show a time relationship, link with a word that makes the time interval clear (during, after, later).

Only you as a writer know the exact relationship between your ideas; link appropriately.

USE CLEAR TRANSITIONS

Transitions guide the reader through your writing and tie your ideas together for him. Your transitions say "go ahead to my next point," "take a detour here for a few moments," "stand still while I illustrate," "contrast that with what I'm going to say now," "let me qualify that with," or "look behind while I remind you where we've been."

Length is not the only determiner in the time it takes someone to read your report or letter; organization and transitional signals have much to do with leading your reader through your ideas quickly. Use signal words and phrases such as those in Figure 19 to cue your reader about where you're taking him next. In addition to these transitional words and phrases, you can repeat key ideas or words to signal your reader. For example:

> ... Their hypothesis was not motivated by nostalgia for past accomplishments, but rather by *concern* for the future.
> A similar *interest* turned up in the reports done ...

> ... Thus, the war had a double effect on the postwar *writings* of our engineers.
> These postwar *writings* contained descriptions of ...

> ... These unsolved *reservations* delayed that experimenting.
> Nevertheless, these *reservations* served as an impetus to related studies in the field of ...

As you edit your work, insert transitions to guide your reader. If you don't lead, the reader may hesitate or get lost along the way.

The Reader's Guide to Your Literature
TRANSITIONS

Adding:
and, again, add to this, in addition, even more, especially, how much more, above all, best of all, most of all, additionally, yet more important, together with this, besides, equally important, further, furthermore, moreover, too, next, first, finally, last, here again

Changing tone or point of view:
at least, for my part, in another sense, as a matter of fact, in fact, in general, of course, as the matter stands, as things are, all this aside

Comparing:
parallel with, comparable to, in the same category, in like manner, in the same way, of the same nature, similarly, likewise, a similar view, equally

Conceding:
certainly, to be sure, granted, true, admittedly, no doubt, doubt-less, this being true, even so, in spite of this, nonetheless
Concluding:
to conclude, finally, lastly, in conclusion, last of all, in brief, in short, as I have said, as noted, in other words, in final analysis, on the whole, in summary, summing up, to sum up
Contrasting:
but, yet, however, nevertheless, on the other hand, on the contrary, for all that, in contrast, by contrast, at the same time, conversely, even so
Excepting:
with this exception, disregarding, excluding, regardless of, exclusive of, irrespective of, omitting this one point
Illustrating:
for example, for instance, for analytical purposes, suppose, to illustrate, to demonstrate, as an illustration, for purposes of clarifying, to clarify, by way of illustration, a case in point, another case, to explain, in other words, that is to say
Indicating Causal Relationships:
thereby, therefore, accordingly, consequently, thus, unfortunately so, as a result, according to, hence, because of this, such being the case, this being true, for this reason, under these circumstances, due to, on such occasions
Indicating Spatial Relationships:
above, below, beneath, overhead, in the foreground, in the background, inside of, outside of, on the exterior, in the interior, under, over, beside, behind, in front of
Qualifying:
although, although this is true, while, notwithstanding, still, furthermore, further, not forgetting
Returning to original point:
to continue, to resume, to return, along with, as I mentioned earlier, now, again, once more, at any rate, returning to my earlier point
Showing purpose:
with this in mind, so, to this end, for this purpose, for this reason

Figure 19

USE CLEAR REFERENCES

The pronouns "this," "that," "it," "they," and "which" are primary villains in unclear references.

Canister pressures were monitored closely, and headspace gas samples were taken in vacutainers whenever the pressure reached approximately 2 psi. *This* was violated during transport of the canisters. (Did they fail to monitor closely while transporting? Did they fail to take gas samples? Did they fail to take gas samples when the pressure was at approximately 2 psi?)
Clear:
". . . Samples were not taken during . . ."

Our campaign to interest others in the use of the company library, causing a more rapid expansion in and of itself, may not benefit the total operation. Like many other areas in Office Services, it has a pressing need. (What has a pressing need—the library or the campaign effort?)
Clear:
. . .The library has a pressing need . . .

Delivery of an additional vacuum pump and porta-power will be required for the project, which has been postponed pending SOC approval. (What has been postponed, the delivery or the project?)
Clear:
Delivery of an additional vacuum pump and porta-power will be required for the project; however, this delivery has been postponed pending SOC approval.

Make sure that a pronoun can stand for only one referent.

PLACE MODIFIERS CORRECTLY

Misplaced words, phrases, and clauses obscure meaning. Notice the difference in meaning in the following sentences when the word "only," a particularly troublesome adverb, is moved around:

Only the operator altered the table in his report about the company's inefficiency.
The operator *only* altered the table in his report about the company's inefficiency.
The operator altered *only* the table in his report about the company's inefficiency.
The operator altered the table *only* in his report about the company's inefficiency.
The operator altered the table in his report about the company's *only* inefficiency.

Misplaced clauses also cause trouble. For example:

There are discrepancies in some of the data *which we are trying to recheck.* (Are they rechecking the discrepancies or all the data?)
Clear:
There are discrepancies, which we are trying to recheck, in some of the data.

Is there nonproprietary documentary information that would help distinguish these samples from possible future ones *that we could have?* (Is the writer asking to be sent information? Or is he asking if there is information available to help them distinguish these samples from future samples they may uncover? If he doesn't get the information, he shouldn't be surprised!)

Clear:
Is there any non-proprietary documentary information that we could have to help distinguish these samples from possible future ones?

A modifying adjective clause or phrase always attaches to the closest noun or pronoun; make sure that close noun or pronoun is the one you intend to describe.

PREFER CONCRETE WORDS AND PHRASES

Words vary in meaning from person to person and from company to company. The interpretation of abstract words and phrases depends on your reader's purposes, his experiences, or his frame of reference—not yours.

Rumor has it that their company's storage *facilities* are completely *inadequate.* (Facilities: Warehouse? Dock? Storage tanks? Filing and cabinet space? Computer storage? *Inadequate:* Size? Location? Construction? Security?)
Plants in *similar* cities have proven successful. (*Similar:* Size? Location? Life-style of clientele? Economic strength? Educational level of population?)

Such words are abstractions; they give multiple meanings. Use a concrete word that gives the correct, precise meaning you intend. Short words are usually the most precise.

Verification	(Proof? Approval? Fact? Check?)
Remuneration	(Salary? Benefit package? Bonus?)
Subsequently	(Next? Later? Therefore?—not a correct mean-

ing, but many writers use the word to mean "therefore")

Configuration	(Symbol? Pattern? Apparatus? Layout?)
Observe	(See? Do? Follow?)

Vague phrases also cause problems. For example:

Can you get these to me *within a few days?*

When I ask class participants to tell me what their habitual response time would be with a request like the one above, their answers range from two to ten days. If the writer of such a statement has no deadline in mind, there's no problem. The irritation comes when the writer *does* have a definite date in mind cloaked behind "within a few days" and the reader responds to his own timetable, a later one.

Granted, you may be able to tell from the context of the memo or letter what "within a few days," "inadequate," "similar," "unsuitable conditions," or "unavoidable delays" mean. But often you cannot.

Let me say a word about jargon here. Vague phrases such as the ones above may have carelessness or courtesy at their source. But vagueness resulting from unnecessary jargon irritates a reader. Why do writers lapse into jargon when a simple, clear statement would communicate the message as well? Some use jargon to impress; others use it out of ignorance, unaware that others don't know what they mean; some use it to hedge or cover up for having nothing to say.

Of course, you must use the jargon of your profession on occasion; a word like "turnkey" contract, or "footage" contract, or "daywork" contract would substitute for a sentence or two of explanation. Chemists, doctors, accountants, lawyers, teachers, and gymnasts all have vocational jargon words useful for expressing complicated ideas to their colleagues. But the key to jargon usage is in my last phrase, "to their colleagues."

I'm perturbed rather than impressed when I go to my doctor with an infection and hear him throw out every medical term he has at his disposal to describe my condition and cure. When he writes a referral letter to another specialist, he can use all the

VAGUE PHRASES

medical jargon he chooses, but I expect to be informed in understandable layman's terms.

People from other departments of your company, managers removed from the specific workings of your office, and clients expect the same from you—simple, clear words. If you don't say what you mean, don't be surprised or angry that you don't get what you want.

USE A CONSISTENT VIEWPOINT

"First person" point of view means using "I" or "we"; the writer talks about himself. In "second person" point of view the writer talks directly to the reader: "You cannot transfer these records." The "you" may be understood as in this sentence: "Do not transfer these records." In "third person" point of view the writer talks *about* someone or something other than himself or the reader: "The company has paid the claim." "Service has been interrupted."

Notice the inconsistency in the point of view in the following memo excerpt:

> Requisitions should be approved by department heads or their designated representatives. Have all Forms 200 filled in and submit them to the Accounting Department.

The first sentence is third person; the second sentence is second person—"you" do something. Therefore, whose responsibility is it to get the requisitions to the Accounting Department? Heads of the departments mentioned in the first sentence? The "you" addressed in the second sentence?

> *Revised:*
> Fill out Form 200, get it approved by a department head or his designated representative, and then submit it to the Accounting Department.

Many writers, however, even when they are consistent about using third person, drop out all the people. Passive voice creates this problem because the "doer" in the sentence hangs on awkwardly and begs to be lopped off the end.

> Arrangements to have these in my office by Friday, February 12, should be announced immediately by each supervisor.

The "by each supervisor" sounds awkward, and the tendency is to omit this information. And therein lies the problem:

> Arrangements to have these in my office by Friday, February 12, should be announced immediately.

In business writing, who does what is usually important to the message. Instructions that mention no person can be deadly—literally. At the very least, such instructions will be ignored or misconstrued. Name a person and be consistent from sentence to sentence about who does what.

Editing your own writing for clarity is difficult; nothing sounds unclear to you because you know what you mean. But when a typist comes to you to question a phrase or organizational detail, when recipients of your memos or letters phone to ask for explanations you thought you gave in your writing, when your instructions are not followed as you specified, take these signals as warnings that you need improvement in this area.

Arrange to have a colleague edit your work before it goes out, and then listen to the questions he raises or the suggestions he makes. If you do the same editing for your friend, the time spent will be a trade-off.

In summary, when editing for clarity: Consider readability; position to indicate emphasis; link to show relationships; use clear transitions; use clear references; place modifiers as close to the noun or pronoun they modify as possible; prefer concrete words and phrases rather than vague ones; use a consistent viewpoint.

To evaluate your mastery of these principles in editing for clarity, do the exercise in Appendix F.

EDIT FOR CONCISENESS

The most frequent complaint I hear from reading executives concerns length of reports and memos. The writer takes seven pages to say what he could say more concisely in three. To cut length saves writing time, reading time, typing time—all translatable into money.

Another benefit is that brevity adds punch. Consider these cliches: "Familiarity breeds contempt." "Pride goes before a fall." "Haste makes waste." "Forewarned is forearmed." These have become cliches because they are strong, precise, concise.

The more words you pour into a sentence, the weaker the message. In a long report, the main ideas often get buried in a mound of details. Good writers know the value of getting to the point.

PREFER ACTIVE- VOICE VERBS

Recall from the "Edit for Grammar" section that all verbs have "voice." In active voice, the subject is the doer of the action of the verb. In passive voice, the subject receives the action of the verb. In addition to length, you may have noticed that passive voice creates a lackluster, stilted, impersonal tone. Thus the term "passive." Active voice, on the hand, sounds alive, personal, demanding. Thus the term "active." A side effect of this passive construction, as mentioned earlier, is the dangling participial phrase.

Then in "Edit for Clarity" I mentioned that passive voice often omits people and that who does what in business writing is usually important. Passive voice comes under attack again because on average, it lengthens sentences by 15 to 50 percent.

Passive:	Separate requisitions should be prepared by each buyer. (eight words)
Active:	Each buyer should prepare separate requisitions. (six words)
Passive:	Variations in canister pressure and air temperatures were accounted for in the calculations by our investigators. (16 words)
Active:	Our investigators accounted for variations in canister pressure and air temperature in their calculations. (14 words)
Passive:	Your prompt attention to this matter will be appreciated. (nine words)
Active:	Please attend to this matter promptly. (six words)
Passive:	It has been concluded by our investigators . . . (seven words)
Active:	Our investigators conclude . . . (three words)

What's the big concern if your sentence has 16 words rather than eight? Nothing—if you write only one sentence.

But if you habitually write in passive voice, you unnecessarily turn a five-paragraph memo into a ten-paragraph one.

Some writers, however, may prefer passive voice because "it sounds more intellectual," or "it sounds more objective," or "business writing has always been done that way." But none of the above is true. Note the personal references and active-voice verbs in the excerpt from Louis Pasteur on fermentation (Figure 20). I could have chosen excerpts from any number of other intellectuals from Francis Bacon to Thomas Paine, excerpts written in active voice with personal pronouns.

Neither does leaving people out of your writing make it more

Louis Pasteur on Fermentation

"The following experiments were undertaken to solve this double problem:—*We* took a double-necked flask, of three litres (five pints) capacity, one of the tubes being curved and forming an escape for the gas; the other one, on the right side (Fig. 1), being furnished with a glass tap. *We* filled this flask with pure yeast water, sweetened with 5 percent of sugar candy, the flask being so full that there was not the least trace of air remaining above the tap or in the escape tube; this artificial wort had, however, been itself aerated. The curved tube was plunged in a porcelain vessel full of mercury, resting on a firm support. In the small cylindrical funnel above the tap, the capacity of which was from 10 cc. to 15 cc. (about half a fluid ounce) *we* caused to ferment, at a temperature of 20° or 25° C (about 75° F), five or six cubic centimetres of the saccharine liquid, by means of a trace of yeast, which multiplied rapidly, causing fermentation, and forming a slight deposit of yeast at the bottom of the funnel above the tap. *We* then opened the tap, and some of the liquid in the funnel entered the flask, carrying with it the small deposit of yeast, which was sufficient to impregnate the saccharine liquid contained in the flask. In this manner it is possible to introduce as small a quantity of yeast as *we* wish, a quantity the weight of which, *we* may say, is hardly appreciable." (Reprinted with permission of the Harvard Classics, copyright 1980, Grolier Enterprises Corp.)

Figure 20. Personal pronouns and active-voice verbs make clear, concise writing.

objective. Haven't you read "third person" passive-voice newspaper or magazine articles that were, without doubt, politically or morally biased? Passive voice does not ensure objectivity, only length.

Finally, just because reports in your company "have always been done that way" doesn't mean that the practice should continue. Aren't new ideas and methods the reasons for promotions? Few will argue with efficiency.

Use of this impersonal passive style is particularly puzzling in an age when businesses advertise their "personal" interest in customers. But more about that in the "Edit for Style" section.

Legitimately, some writers will defend passive voice, saying that first person sounds immodest, that lesser men should not dare refer to themselves. Of course, if you are describing your own work, using "I" repeatedly gets monotonous and may sound pompous. I'll get to other purposes for passive voice a little later.

How do you convert passive voice to active voice? Use the personal pronoun when necessary. For example:

Passive: Several steps are being implemented by our department to expedite consistent service for ordering. (14 words)

Active: We are implementing several steps to expedite consistent service for ordering. (11 words)

Passive: This equipment should be examined for damage. (seven words)

Active: Examine this equipment for damage. (five words)

A second way to convert passive voice to active voice is to make the "doer" at the end of the sentence (usually the object of the preposition "by") the subject of the sentence.

Passive: Additional pile penetration may also be obtained by *removal of the soil plug.* (13 words)

Active: *Removing the soil plug* allows additional pile penetration. (eight words)

Passive: It will have been determined *by Corporate Headquarters* what commodities and services will be purchased locally. (16 words)

Active: *Corporate Headquarters* will determine what commodities and services will be purchased locally. (12 words)

Passive: The precipitate was separated *by the vacuum filtering.* (8 words)

Active: *Vacuum filtering* separated the precipitate. (five words)

Can passive voice be all bad? Of course not. Continual use of active-voice verbs would be monotonous and at times pompous, as I mentioned earlier. Second, passive voice is useful for hedging: "It has been decided that incentive awards will no longer be made." Who decided? No one is to blame. Third, passive voice sounds courteous: "A mistake was made." You don't want to sound overbearing or accusatory to your client.

Finally, passive voice can shift emphasis to the results when the "doer" is unimportant: "All employees were evacuated before the explosion." By whom or what is unimportant.

Thus, passive-voice sentences can be useful on occasion, but prefer active voice for conciseness.

DIG BURIED VERBS OUT OF NOUN PHRASES

To shorten some sentences, all you need do is locate the legitimate verbs hiding in nouns. Words ending in *-ion, -tion, -ing, -ment, -ent, -ance, -ence, -age, -ancy, -ency, -tian,* and *-ology* signal that you've found a noun. Take away that ending and use the good verb in another of its purer forms:

> I still have available details from the administrative meeting and will advise specific data for your use in *arrangement* and *solicitation* of proposals. (23 words)
> becomes . . .
> I still have available details from the administrative meeting and will advise specific data to *arrange* and *solicit* proposals. (18 words)

> This will provide for the *elimination* of the time for *review* and *comparison* of bids. (15 words)
> becomes . . .
> This will *eliminate* time for *reviewing* and *comparing* bids. (nine words)

> They *experienced a reduction* in construction time by the *initiation of slip-dredging operations.* (13 words)
> becomes . . .
> They *reduced* construction time by *slip dredging.* (seven words)

> We have designed the operational auditing course for *the training of* auditors *in conducting an independent review and evaluation* of policies. (21 words)
> becomes . . .
> We have designed the operational auditing course *to train* auditors *to review and evaluate* policies. (15 words)

Digging out buried verbs shortens sentences and adds impact.

AVOID ADJECTIVE AND ADVERB CLUTTER

"Familiarity breeds contempt." These are words of fact, or at least they sound like fact. Nouns and verbs bear the weight of your message. "Too much familiarity often breeds unwanted contempt." These are words of opinion, adjectives and adverbs. Most business writing should sound factual, not opinionated.

> You will *probably* gain the background you need. ("Probably" is opinion; it weakens the impact.)

> When all proposals are received, they can be *leisurely* evaluated on a *truly* comparative basis.
> When all proposals are received, they can be evaluated on a comparative basis. (No opinion words, sounds factual.)

Granted, adjectives and adverbs can add emphasis or provide a trapdoor: "This report is *completely* worthless." The adverb here adds emphasis. "This new machine will *probably* be more expensive to operate." The adverb hedges, providing an outlet that an outright claim would not.

Unless you have a specific purpose in mind, however, for such words, develop the habit of writing with nouns and verbs, omitting adjectives and adverbs where possible.

CUT CIRCUMLOCUTIONS

Besides adjective and adverb clutter, business writing reeks with "fat." Trimming circumlocutions (cliches, redundancies, little-word padding, weak-verb padding) will make your writing emphatic and crisp.

Some writers, though, have problems recognizing the "fat" in their own work. They use the same phraseology in form letter after form letter, never giving thought to more effective wording. Of course, cliches stand out in others' writing: "Facts and figures." "At this point in time." "Enclosed herewith please find." Finding such in your own work is more exacting. If you feel the phrases "roll off your tongue" "with little or no effort" (as the last two phrases just rolled off mine), that's a clue that you're using a cliche.

Sentences that incorporate redundant words and ideas are harder to recognize. For instance, "continue on." To continue means to go on; when you add the "on," you're stuttering. "If you can't spell 'accommodations,' look it up in the dictionary and check it." The entire last idea is redundant. "If you can't spell 'accommodations,' check the dictionary."

102

Little-word padding also clutters and dilutes messages.

This proves true only *in the case* where more than three tests were performed.
This proves true only where more than three tests were performed.

Our experience in handling large-scale programs is particularly suited for this *type of* project.
Our experience in handling large-scale programs is particularly suited for this project.

The number of shifts worked could be attributed to *various factors such as* market size, labor problems, and management philosophy.
The number of shifts worked could be attributed to market size, labor problems, and management philosophy.

The following symbols are used *in all portions of* this report.
The following symbols are used *throughout* this report.

The attached Form 2138 is for *your use in* developing the necessary data.
The attached Form 2138 is for developing the necessary data.

Attached is a copy of the form *which must be completed in advance* before *they will give us the service.*
Attached is a copy of the form *to be completed* before *service.*

Examine Figure 21 for your "pet" circumlocutions. Recognition is half the solution in stripping them from your writing.

In short, prefer active-voice verbs, dig buried verbs from noun phrases, avoid adjective and adverb clutter, and cut circumlocutions. Writing long sentences is like adding water to tea; the more words, the weaker the message.

To evaluate your mastery of this section's material, edit the exercise in Appendix G.

CIRCUMLOCUTIONS
(Cliches, Redundancies, Little-Word Padding)

in the amount of	for
for the purpose of	for
in reference to	about
with reference to	about
in connection with	about

with regard to	about
in regard to	about
pertaining to	to
to be in a position to	to
in order to	to
in order that	to
with a view toward	to
for the express purpose of	to
in the event that	if
if it should turn out that	if
if it is assumed that	if
inasmuch as	as
in spite of the fact that	although
with the result that	so
on account of the fact that	since, because
for the reason that	since, because
in view of the fact that	since, because
to say nothing of	and
in view of the foregoing circumstances	therefore
it is apparent therefore that	hence
along the lines of	like
in the nature of	like
by means of	by, using
until such time as you	until you
with the exception of	except
the question as to whether	whether
in conjunction with	with
if at all possible	if possible
in all other cases	otherwise
a sufficient number of	enough
in the vicinity of	near
it would seem that	apparently, probably
it would thus appear that	apparently, probably
in a satisfactory manner	satisfactorily
on a regular basis	regularly
by the same token	similarly
in most cases	usually
in all cases	always, all
not infrequently	often
until such time as	until
a great length of time	longer
at a later date	later
at an early date	soon
at this point in time	now

at the present time	now
at this precise moment in time	now
in this day and age	now
after this has been done	then
on two separate occasions	twice
it may well be that	perhaps
during the time that	while
a large number of	many
a great deal of	much
a proportion of	some
a number of	some, several
few in number	few
a small number of	few
cost the sum of	cost
during the month of April	in April
during the year of 1968	in 1968
red in color	red
large in size	large
cylindrical in shape	cylindrical
a distance of 80 yards	80 yards
not longer than 25,000 words in length	no more than 25,000 words
comings and goings	travels
facts and figures	data
an oral presentation	talk
on an experimental basis	by experiment
as an extra added bonus	as a bonus
of a reversible nature	reversible
totally demolished	demolished
put off	delay, postpone
continue on	continue
continue to remain	remain
refer back to	refer to
aimed at	for
consolidated together	consolidated
count on	count
check on	check
later on	later
prior to	before
seal off	seal
grouped together	grouped
in between	between
try out	try
open up	open

pay back	repay
send around	distribute
duly noted	noted
completely surrounded	surrounded
conclusive proof	proof
in actual fact	in fact
deliberately chosen	chosen
in my own personal opinion	in my opinion
on pages 2-10 inclusive	on pages 2-10
in two equal halves	in two halves
symptoms indicative of	symptoms
temporary loan	loan
one of the most unique	unique
he went on to say	continued
conduct an investigation into	investigate
bring to conclusion	finish, conclude
are found to be in agreement with	agree
carry out experiments	experiment
which goes under the name of	called
take into consideration	consider
has an ability to	can
make an examination of	examine
undertake a study of	study
afford an opportunity to	allow
proved to be	were
make an adjustment to	adjust
may possibly go	may go
not actually true	untrue
make the statement that	says
for the construction of	in making
will be of assistance in	will help
will be an aid to	will aid
give positive encouragement to	encourage
have been shown to be	are
you are in fact quite correct	you are right
made our departure	departed
were in attendance	attended
extended an invitation	invited
fully cognizant of	aware
hold in abeyance	postpone
put in an appearance	appeared
are in receipt of	received
they are in fact	they are
please arrange to return	return

we are not in a position to	we cannot
may we suggest that you	please
we will take steps to	we will
enclosed herewith please find	enclosed is
the reason for this is because	the reason is
the reason is due to the fact that	the reason is
the reason why we	the reason we
I tentatively suggest	I suggest

Figure 21. Trim the fat from your writing.

EDIT FOR STYLE

Style reflects individuality; it is your personal logo. Some people write with a warm, personal, flowing sytle, while others have a formal, impersonal, stilted way with words. The trend in today's business writing is away from "stuffed shirt" writing.

How do you develop a pleasing countenance on paper?

VARY SENTENCE PATTERN AND LENGTH

Variety in sentence pattern is to writing what voice inflection is to speech. A steady diet of any one construction makes for boring reading:

Monotonous:
Note the attached charts, and please submit to me a written report explaining irregularities. Obviously, corrective actions were ineffective, and I cannot accept this situation. You will need to give me a written report of all past financial procedures, and also you will need to delineate new ones to establish and maintain effective controls. I will review your corrective proposals personally, and I would like for you to be conversant with the appropriate publications. These proposals should be in my office no later than October 21, and our conference will follow within the next few days. (Sentence patterns: compound, compound, compound, compound, compound.)

A page of this pitter-pat, pitter-pat, pitter-pat would put a reader to sleep. The writer has joined every other independent clause with "and." Note the difference in the following revision:

Revised:

Note the attached charts, and please submit to me a written report explaining irregularities. Obviously corrective actions were ineffective. Because I cannot accept this situation, you will need to give me a written report of all past financial procedures and delineate new ones to establish and maintain effective controls. When I review your corrective proposals personally, I would like for you to be conversant with the appropriate publications. These proposals should be in my office no later than October 21, and our conference will follow within the next few days. (Sentence patterns: compound, simple, complex, compound.)

A little editing for variety's sake goes a long way.

In addition to variety in pattern, vary length. Follow a 30-word sentence with a five-word sentence. The jolt will make your reader sit up and pay attention.

REVISE WEAK VERBS

Spice bland writing with potent verbs. Some writers make a timid attempt to jump into their subjects with weak verb constructions such as "there is," "there are," "it is," "it was."

Weak:	There are problems in remaining static.
Strong:	Remaining static presents problems.
Weak:	There were some objections voiced during the meeting.
Strong:	Some voiced objections during the meeting.
Weak:	It has been firmly established by previous research that this machine will improve the operation.
Strong:	Previous research firmly establishes that this machine will improve the operation.
Weak:	It is difficult to maintain movable equipment.
Strong:	Maintaining movable equipment is difficult.

Of course, not all such weak verb constructions can be revised; alternatives may sound awkward. But prefer a strong verb to command the reader's attention.

PREFER A PERSONAL, CONVERSATIONAL TONE

To grasp a clear understanding of "tone" in writing, imagine how the same words would sound if spoken. Besides the usual meanings of tone (confident, pleasant, angry, sarcastic, aggressive), consider the personal and impersonal tone.

Tone is the dress of your letters. You dress differently on various occasions; you write differently on different occasions. Study the following variations:

Informal:
You all are pretty much aware that one of the main themes for division managers will be overseeing and controlling gas consumption by your employees. This theme will be hammered at hard and heavy throughout the year and, I am sure, in the years to come. It will be up to you to set stringent objectives to help your people better plan their schedules and to see that they operate company cars efficiently. I'm convinced that a number of our people do not give the same attention to the company cars as they would to their own family cars when they have to buy gasoline out of their own pockets.

Formal:
As you are aware, one of the main objectives for division managers will be supervising and regulating gas consumption by employees. The company will repeatedly emphasize automobile economy throughout the years to come. Managers must set stringent objectives to help employees better plan their schedules and use company cars efficiently. Such objectives should encourage employees to give company cars the same careful attention as they give their personal cars.

Pompous:
As all management is cognizant, one of the principal objectives for division managers will be the supervision and regulation of gasoline consumption by personnel. Economic and efficient usage of automobiles will be a recurring concern in the years to come, and it is incumbent that stringent objectives be established for all personnel with due respect to efficient juxtapositions of appointments within the same geographical region and to the prudent utilization of company vehicles. These objectives should incorporate incentives for personnel to render company transportation the same meticulous attention as would be afforded personal vehicles.

Of course, minor revisions in the second, formal version (for instance, omission of all pronouns) make the writing slightly less or more formal.

In general, to choose the appropriate style for a report, letter or memo, consider how you would express your ideas in conversations with the same reader or readers. But be careful to omit repe-

LETTERS SHOULD GET PERSONAL!

titious details, choppy sentences, and grammatical errors that
you may use in speaking.

Also follow these tips to make your writing friendly:

- *Use a person's name and spell it correctly.* "Dear Mr. Murphy" sounds more cordial than "Dear Sir." And if you would do so in conversation, call a person by his or her first name. A phone call to a receptionist will give you the correct spelling of name and title. A missing or misspelled name tells the reader he isn't too important to you.

- *Avoid opening with a warm-up drill.* "This letter acknowledges receipt of your December 12 letter requesting information about the Hite Survey taken in the field on . . ." sets up an impersonal, stuffy style. This letter acknowledges? Why don't you? Summarizing all past correspondence suggests the reader's memory or files or both aren't too good. Say instead, "I have received your letter of December 13 and am happy to forward the Hite Survey information you wanted."

- *Include pleasantries.* Mention upcoming holidays, refer to past conversations, or express congratulations or praise when in order. But be sincere; overstatement sounds sarcastic and artificial.

- *Watch "fight" words.* "Mistaken," "failed," "overlooked," "misled," or "ignored" trigger an adverse gut reaction. If you're writing to request corrective action, such words will thwart your purpose.

- *Include courtesy words.* Words like "please," "appreciate," or "thank you" are never out of order.

- *Use simple words, not pompous ones.* Dignity, closely aligned with simplicity, means a writing style appropriate to subject matter, void of colloquialisms and grammatical errors. Pomposity, on the other hand, means excessively ornate or elevating, exhibiting self-importance. (In selecting jewelry you know that the most ornate is not always the most expensive.) This is not to say that you should avoid complex words altogether—especially if the complex word says exactly what you mean. But don't overlook the simple word in an effort to sound dignified. A writer who continually uses pompous words and phrases when simple ones will do is an amusement to his reader.

- *Never tell someone what he thinks or feels.* Writers of humor know better than to tell a reader, "The funniest thing happened . . . ." The reader is set up for disappointment. Likewise, a statement such as, "We all know you will enjoy making this trip to the East Coast" may bring the reaction, "Oh, yeah?"

- *Don't be too arbitrary.* When possible, give sufficient reason for actions or requests. People with a reason tend to cooperate better—even when they don't agree.

- *Don't be too patronizing.* Do not give unnecessary explanations or talk down to your reader.
- *Don't be too indifferent or careless.* Answer all the reader's questions promptly; avoid choosing details you think he needs while omitting others as privileged information.
- *Avoid cliches.* They not only add length, as mentioned earlier, but also mark you as a lazy thinker. For example:

> If you will be kind enough to
>
> Pursuant to our meeting
>
> The fact of the matter is
>
> Under separate cover
>
> We beg to advise
>
> We take pleasure in
>
> After due consideration
>
> Enclosed herewith please find
>
> In reference to the matter of
>
> Your letter at hand
>
> As per your letter
>
> At the present writing

Such cliches make your writing sound like a form letter; someone merely touched the "print" button. Certainly, form letters have a place in the business world. But when you want to influence your reader favorably, give careful thought to original phraseology and take time to address his special concerns in a personal way.

In summary, when editing for style, vary sentence patterns and length, change weak verbs to stronger ones, and prefer a conversational, personal tone.

After reading this book, you may be wondering: Should I try to write memos, letters, and reports at all? That question should not be taken lightly. Before you take out pen and paper or pick up the dictaphone, consider the following reasons for putting your message in writing: Is the person too difficult to reach by phone? Will my reader need to keep the written message for later reference and reminder? If I'm writing to several readers, do they all *really* need this information? Do I need a permanent record of this communication?

Much business writing does not and cannot stand on its own; the writer must interpret his message in person or by phone and then send a confirming memo or letter.

But when you must write and when your writing must work, review and practice the five steps detailed here for effective communication.

BIBLIOGRAPHY

Barrass, Robert. *Scientists Must Write*. New York: Halstead, 1978.

Brogan, John A. *Clear Technical Writing*. New York: McGraw-Hill, 1973.

Brown, Leland. *Effective Business Report Writing*. Englewood Cliffs, N.J.: Prentice-Hall, 1973.

Callihan, E. L. *Grammar for Journalists*. Radnor, Pa.: Chilton, 1979.

Clapp, John Mantle. *Accountants' Writing*. New York: Ronald Press, 1948.

Dawe, Jessamon, and Lord William Jackson, Jr. *Functional Business Communications*. Englewood Cliffs, N. J.: Prentice-Hall, 1974.

Flesch, Rudolf. *How to Write, Speak and Think*. New York: Harper & Brothers, 1951.

Gunning, Robert. *The Technique of Clear Writing*. New York: McGraw-Hill, 1968.

Hughson, Roy V., ed. *Effective Communications for Engineers*. New York: McGraw-Hill, 1974.

Hutchison, Lois Irene. *Standard Handbook for Secretaries*. New York: McGraw-Hill, 1969.

Joseph, Albert, *Put It in Writing*. Cleveland: International Writing Institute, 1979.

A Manual of Style, 12th ed., rev. Chicago: University of Chicago Press; 1969.

Mathes, J. C., and Stevenson, Dwight W. *Designing Technical Reports*. New York: Bobbs-Merrill, 1976.

Mitchell, Evan. *The Businessman's Guide to Letter-Writing and to the Law on Letters*. London: Business Books, 1970.

114

Murray, Melba. *Engineered Report Writing.* Tulsa: Arco, 1969.

Owen, J. W., and Davies, J. *Business Punctuation.* London: Pitman, 1974.

Sheff, Alexander L., and Ingalls, Edna. *How to Write Letters for All Occasions.* Garden City, N. Y.: Doubleday, 1971.

Sklare, Arnold B. *The Technician Writes: A Guide to Basic Technical Writing.* San Francisco: Boyd & Fraser, 1971.

Strunk, William, Jr., and White, E. B. *The Elements of Style, Third Edition.* New York: Macmillan, 1979.

Taintor, Sarah Augusta, and Monro, Kate M. *The Secretary's Handbook.* New York: Macmillan, 1969.

Tracy, Raymond C., and Jennings, Harold L. *Writing for Industry.* Chicago American Technical Society, 1973.

Weiss, Allen. *Write What You Mean: A Handbook of Business Communication.* New York: AMACOM, 1977.

APPENDIXES

APPENDIX A

THE FIVE STEPS FOR EFFECTIVE WRITING APPLIED TO *WOULD YOU PUT THAT IN WRITING?*

Step One: Consider Your Audience for the Proper Angle

Anyone who writes or reads reports, letters, and memos—both technical and nontechnical.

Interests—reducing writing and reading time, shortening report length, organizing details and data, influencing through tone, and developing personal style. Must see practical use on the job.

Knowledge—probably average knowledge of "academic" writing do's and don'ts. Possibly foggy on grammatical terms.

Step Two: Anticipate Special Problems in Your Reader's Reaction

1. Some have the idea that "just getting the message across" is sufficient, so I'll need to impress upon them the importance of good writing.
2. Some may have a negative attitude about writing.
3. Some may resist new ideas because of "academic" training or misunderstanding about that training.

Consider these reactions and problems in the first chapter, or the reader may not finish the book. Put the grammar section before the other editing sections, so the reader can refresh himself on terms I'll be using in later sections on clarity, conciseness, and style.

Step Three: Outline the Message Functionally
Basic format for report, letter and memos:

What's the message?	Good writing requires training. Poor writing costs companies much time and money.
What action next?	I recommend five steps for effective reports, letters, and memos.
Who, when, where, why, how details?	Who—anyone who writes technical or nontechnical material. When—N/A. Where—N/A. Why—to save money and time. How—state the five steps, giving explanation and examples to help the reader apply each step to his own writing projects.
Optional evidence?	Samples of work from these steps as they apply to this book. Quizzes and answers for readers who want to test mastery of the book's contents.

APPENDIX B

RANDOM LIST FOR *WOULD YOU PUT THAT IN WRITING?*

Problems in writing—use workshop participants' comments
Illustration of two kinds of drivers
Objectives in writing—clarity, image, cost, conciseness
Examples of unclear writing, unreadable sample
Gunning's Fog Index
Five Steps in Writing will be main outline
Linking to show proper relationships
Emphatic positions in the sentence, paragraph, body of letter
Use sentence No. 16 from my evaluation exercise
Avoid warm-up drills in letters
Tone—personal and impersonal
Cliches, easy to recognize
Include quizzes and answers after each editing checklist
Redundancies
Little-word padding: "type of"; "for the purpose of"; "various factors"; "for your use in"
Digging out buried verbs
Use short sentences
Mr. Steel's comment about too much reading for executives
Prefer active voice; avoid passive voice—adds length, sounds stilted, unclear, dangling verbal
"There is," "it is" constructions—weak
Clear references
Good transitions

Place modifiers close to nouns they modify, also danglers
Matching data on index cards
Labeling cards, sorting into piles
Dictate or type?
Content—angle, authority, paragraphing, headings, accuracy
Grammar—dangling verbals, punctuation, fragments, subject-verb agreement, pronoun antecedents
Spelling—hyphens, apostrophes
Repetition
Misused words
Tense changes unnecessarily—show when necessary
Consistent viewpoint—especially when writing instructions
Commas, quotes, dashes, semicolons, colons
When to quote
Special problems in holding reader's interest
How to find reader's interest
Going through several readers for report approval
Why outline—quicker, organize, interruptions, less revising
Logical arrangement of different types of reports and letters
Random listing, reviewing outline to shuffle ideas into place
Ask supervisor for approval before you write
Personality problems in getting approval of report
Skepticism about your conclusions
Basic format for memo—give the "why" first
Basic format for report—conclusions first
Basic format for letter—the same as for report
Allow plenty of time for editing
Poor academic training or incorrect ideas have caused poor business writing—prepositions at end of sentence, paragraph length, etc.
Professors, captive audience, gave you benefit of the doubt

APPENDIX C

GRAMMAR GLOSSARY

absolute
a group of words grammatically unrelated to the rest of the sentence; begins with a noun or pronoun; differs from a clause in that it does not have a complete verb
(*The reports completed*, we left early.)

adjective
describes, points out, or limits a noun or a pronoun
(a, the, black, difficult, provocative)

adverb
tells how, when, where, why, or how much about a verb, adjective, or another adverb
(much, excessively, cautiously, later)

antecedent
a word to which a later word refers
(The *plan, which* is highly workable, can be initiated immediately.)

appositive
an inserted explanation; can be a word, phrase, or clause; usually follows the noun or pronoun it explains
(The fact *that we left early* can't be argued.)
(The target area, *the Saudia jobsite*, can . . .)

clause
a group of words containing a subject and a predicate

independent
a clause that makes sense alone
(After the job estimate was turned in, *he proceeded on schedule*.)

dependent	does not express a complete thought and must depend on the independent clause for full meaning (*After the job estimate was turned in*, he proceeded on schedule.)
complement	follows a linking verb (is, are, was, were, become, looks, seems, etc.) and completes the meaning of the verb
subjective	renames or describes the subject of the sentence (Mr. Smith is president.) (Mr. Smith became angry.)
objective	tells about the direct object (He considered the project a *failure*.)
conjunction	a word to join other words or groups of words
coordinate	joins elements of equal rank (and, or, nor, for, but, yet, so)
subordinate	joins elements of unequal rank (since, if, although, because, as)
correlative	conjunctions used in pairs (either-or, neither-nor, whether-or not, both-and, not-but, though-yet)
expletive	a word having nothing grammatically to do with the rest of the sentence; often introduces the subject (*There* is nothing more we can do.) (*It* is difficult to do these tests.)
fragment	an incomplete sentence; usually incomplete because the group of words contains no verb (All procedures outlined in the first 10 pages of the report describing the absorption processes.)
interjection	a word expressing strong or sudden feeling; grammatically unrelated to the rest of the sentence (Oh! Cheers! No!)

modifier	a word or group of words that describes or limits another word (*difficult* task) (plan *which was inadequate*)
mood	
indicative	verb makes a statement of fact (My memo confirms the opinion.)
subjunctive	verb states idea, event, or condition contrary to fact (If he would let me, I'd resign.)
imperative	verb states a command (Sign this memo.)
noun	the name of a person, place, thing, or idea (Mr. Brown, warehouse, schedule, freedom.)
noun of address	the person to whom the rest of the sentence is addressed (*Mr. Smith*, I can't thank you enough.)
number	refers to noun, pronoun, or verb; indicates whether one or more is meant (building, building*s*; indicate*s*, indicate; mine, ours)
restrictive	restricts the meaning of the main clause; essential to the meaning (Replace only the tubes *that have been damaged.*) (tells which tubes)
nonrestrictive	adds information, but nonessential to the sentence meaning (You must replace all the tubes, *which will be rather costly.*)
object	a noun or a pronoun that follows a complete (transitive) verb
direct	a word that receives the action of the verb (Brown injected the *solution* into the samples.)
indirect	the receiver of the direct object (We gave the *job* our best efforts.)
prepositional	a noun or a pronoun that follows the preposition and is linked to some other word by the preposition

(He monitored the valve *throughout the day*.)

(He went *into the warehouse* unescorted.)

parallelism   sentence elements in like structure

(He looked *in the closet, on the shelf,* and *in the desk*.) (all prepositional phrases)

(The manager demanded the following: *reduction in labor charges; change in shipping procedures; improvement in delivery service*.) (all nouns followed by prepositional phrases)

parenthetical element   a word, phrase, clause or sentence that has no grammatical relationship with the rest of the sentence; may be set off by commas, dashes, or parentheses

(I believe—*and this is strictly a personal opinion*—that he should be fired.)

(We have two choices, *to postpone the survey or cancel it*, and neither one is satisfactory.)

phrase   a group of words not having a subject or a predicate

(in the beginning; old, faulty repair; having finished early)

predicate   that which tells something about the subject

(The engineers *have been satisfied with the results of the tests*.)

preposition   a word to show the relationship between its object and some other word in the sentence

(in, at, about, as, between, during, except, of, on; *in* the box, *between* the men)

pronoun   a word substituted for a noun

personal   indicates a person (I, you, they)

demonstrative   points out (this, that, these, those)

relative   relates an adjective clause to its antecedent

	(who, whom, whose, what, that)
interrogative	asks a question (who, what, which)
indefinite	does not stand for a definite person, place, thing, or idea
	(someone, few, some, none, all, both)
reflexive	refers to the subject (myself, himself)
run-on sentence	two or more sentences incorrectly written as one
	(He could not quote the salary, therefore, all the applicants felt they had wasted their time.) (The first comma should be replaced by a semicolon or a period.)
sentence	a group of related words expressing a complete thought and containing a subject and a predicate
simple	contains one subject and one predicate; either or both may be compound
	(Two inspectors and surveyors left and returned twice during the day.)
compound	contains two or more independent clauses
	(The representative called on the company, but he could not sell our services.)
complex	contains one dependent clause and one independent clause
	(When the pressure falls, cut off the machine immediately.)
compound-complex	contains two or more independent clauses and one or more dependent clauses
	(Show me the reports when they come in, but don't forward them until I've checked with his supervisor.)
subject	part of the sentence which names what is talked about
	(*The tubing in the front* is worn out.)
tense	property of verbs that indicates time of the action

present	*investigate* today
past	*investigated* yesterday
future	*will investigate* tomorrow
present perfect	*has investigated* several times
past perfect	*had investigated* before you called
future perfect	*will have investigated* by this time next week
verb	a word to show action or state of being (stops, fills, aids, concludes, pressurizes, is, seems, becomes, struck, was)
verbal	verbs acting as other parts of speech
gerund	verb + -ing, used as a noun (*Testing* is going slowly.)
participle	verb + -ing or -ed, used as an adjective (*Testing the pipes*, he could not turn his back to the meter.)
infinitive	to + verb, used as a noun, adjective, or adverb (*To test* the pipes requires three hours.) (Caps *to stop* the leakage are hard to find.) (He rearranged the charts *to show* the results in optimum light.)
voice	a form of the verb that indicates who or what does the action or receives the action
active	when the subject is the actor in the sentence (The tests *show* pollution.) (The subject, "tests," acts—"show.")
passive	when the subject receives the action in the sentence (Pollution *was shown* by the tests.) (The subject, "pollution," receives the action—"was shown.")

APPENDIX D

ANSWERS TO THE SPELLING QUIZ

accessible, acessible
accomodate, accommodate
accurate, acurrate
achieve, acheive
allotted, alloted
analyze, analize
antequated, antiquated
apparatus, aparratus
arguement, argument
bulletin, bulliten
buoyant, bouyant
category, catagory
changeable, changable
commitment, committment
concensus, consensus
controlled, controled
definite, definate
dependent, dependant
description, discreption
descrepancy, discrepancy
dispel, dispell
embarrass, embarass
exceed, excede
existence, existance
exorbitant, exhorbitant
fourty, forty

insistent, insistant
mecanics, mechanics
mileage, milage
ninety, ninty
ocassionally, occasionally
occurred, occured
occurrence, occurence
parallel, paralell
perform, preform
permanent, permenant
perserverance, perseverance
personnel, personel
precede, preceed
privilege, privelege
proceedure, procedure
procede, proceed
quandary, quandery
porportion, proportion
recede, receed
receive, recieve
repetition, repitition
separate, seperate
seize, sieze
sieve, seive
similar, similiar
succeed, succede

126

<u>superintendent</u>, superintendant
supercede, <u>supersede</u>
<u>inadvertent</u>, inadvertant
indispensible, <u>indispensable</u>
<u>judgment</u>, judgement
<u>license</u>, licence

<u>maintenance</u>, maintanence
<u>technique</u>, techneque
<u>transferred</u>, transfered
<u>vacuum</u>, vaccuum
<u>whether</u>, wheather

APPENDIX E

GRAMMAR QUIZ

Mark "C" beside correct sentences. Label the errors in the remaining sentences.

1. Using the figures from the same quarter last year, it can be predicted that sales will dip about 10 percent.
2. All policies containing explicit procedures have been rescinded. Although such policies have been considered necessary to the safe operation of our plant.
3. Actual cash value at the time of replacements are the figures we should budget for next year.
4. This was the maximum amount of oxygen, therefore, it had been absorbed to the following degree.
5. The shale remained in large pieces and is easily picked out.
6. It's true value decreases with addition of the liquid.
7. Smith seems knowledgeable and is eager to begin the project: interviewing field foremen, ordering the necessary equipment, and construction of the initial foundation.
8. I've been assigned five very time consuming projects in the past six months.
9. The proposal's defeat centers around Brown misleading all the board members.
10. Each supervisor should inform his managers of the new time schedule, and they should post sign-out sheets near the schedule sheets.

Answers (all sentences are incorrect):

1. Dangling verbal—" . . . we can predict . . ."
2. Fragment—put a comma after "rescinded," and attach the last clause to the first clause (which is already a complete sentence).
3. Subject-verb agreement—"cash values are," or "cash value . . . is . . . the figure . . ."
4. Run-on sentence—must have semicolon before "therefore," or make two sentences.
5. Tense change—"remained . . . was," or "remains . . . is . . ."
6. Its—"it's" means it is.
7. Parallelism—". . . constructing the initial foundation."
8. Hyphenate two adjectives that precede a noun: "time-consuming . . ."
9. Possessive form before a gerund—"Brown's misleading . . ."
10. Pronoun agreement—"he should post . . ." If the writer is referring to the staff, he should repeat the noun: ". . . and the managers should post . . ."

APPENDIX F

EXERCISE ON CLARITY

Identify the clarity problems and try to correct them:

1. Attached are brief technical proposals for the determinations of several trace elements in coal liquefaction products and samples of their corresponding feed coals. They could be sent to Mound Lab next week.

2. Accounting has submitted this report to management consistently six weeks late. Arrangements should be made to forward future reports of this nature by the 15th day of each new quarter.

3. These tanks should be monitored continually and the couplings adjusted every two hours or when the pressure reaches the above charted points.

4. The discovery could be of vital importance in purchasing the drilling equipment for the recovery wells, our engineers conclude.

5. The amount of chemical used in the treatment depends on the severity of the fracture system, its permeability distribution, and the maximum injection pressure to be obtained at the end of the treatment. This cannot be overemphasized in your procedures.

6. The proposal on the new investigative procedure was the primary problem, which Joseph mentioned in his letter.

7. An interesting fact is that a floor-load study was done on the office, and there is a section of shelving that weighs about 300 pounds per square foot.

Answers:

1. Referent for "They"? "These proposals (or samples) could . . ."

    Linking word "and"—Are the samples attached?

    Verb tense—"could be sent"? Is this a possibility or is the writer suggesting that they be sent?

    Passive voice—Who should send them?

2. Misplaced modifier—"consistently submitted"

    Passive voice—Who should make the arrangements?

    Vague phrase—"of this nature" (late reports or quarterly reports?)

    Vague date—15th working day or calendar day? Fiscal or calendar quarter?

3. Passive voice—Who should monitor? (Maybe it would be clear from the context and maybe it wouldn't.)

    Linking word—"and"—Isn't the "adjusting" a result of the "monitoring"?

    Linking word—"or"—Is it *either* every two hours *or* when the pressure reaches the charted points? Or will the pressure reach those points every two hours?

    Clear: Monitor these tanks continually, adjusting the couplings either every two hours or when the pressure reaches the above charted points.

4. Position of emphasis—"Our engineers conclude that the. . ." ("Our engineers conclude" hangs on.)

5. Unclear reference—To what does "they" refer? The amount of chemical? One of the items in the series? The relationship between the chemical amount and the three criteria?

    Unclear reference—"its" The fracture system? The well?

6. Dangling modifier or unclear reference—"which"—The proposal? The problem? The procedure?

7. Vague word—"interesting"—Is this a heavy or a light load?

    Improper linking word—This message should be expressed in one clause. "A floor-load study done on the office showed that we have a section of shelving that weighs about 300 pounds per square foot."

APPENDIX G

EXERCISE ON CONCISENESS

Revise these sentences by changing passive voice to active voice, digging out buried verbs, and cutting wasted words.

1. At such time as this program becomes available and economically feasible, management will take steps to delineate the procedures to be followed by each department head in implementing the program in his particular division. (34 words)
2. It should be noted that this opinion addresses only consideration of issues under federal and related Texas laws which are pertinent to gas and gas contracts. (26 words)
3. Utilization of these forms by each department head in the compilation of his department's findings with regard to the Atlanta plant will result in a more efficient and easily assembled final report. (32 words)
4. The efficiency with which an operation utilizes its available equipment is an influential factor in productivity. (16 words)
5. The first two steps would be the appointment of a representative of each subsidiary and the selection of a person to be the coordinator. (24 words)

Suggested revisions:

1. When this program becomes available and economically feasible, management will delineate the procedures for each department head to implement the program. (21 words)

132

2. This opinion addresses only issues under federal and Texas laws pertinent to gas and gas contracts. (16 words)
3. Each department head's using these forms to compile his Atlanta plant findings will result in a more efficient final report. (20 words)
4. Efficiency in using equipment influences productivity. (six words)
5. The first two steps are to appoint a representative of each subsidiary and to select a coordinator. (17 words)